Praise for *Now Is the Way*

"This perfectly timed book is the antidote to our overwhelmed, distracted, and anxiety-ridden modern world. Cory directs us to the present moment with clarity and ease. Read this book and enjoy finding your bliss in the only place it resides . . . right now."

—EMILY FLETCHER, AUTHOR OF *STRESS LESS, ACCOMPLISH MORE*
AND FOUNDER OF ZIVA MEDITATION

"This honest, hilarious, kind, wise, and extremely readable guide to presence, to NOW, is priceless and may well be the most important book you own. It has been a daily companion, guiding me back to reality, to what's actually happening, reeling me back to my breath, reminding me to relax, and making me laugh along the way."

—DEVENDRA BANHART, AUTHOR OF *WEEPING GANG BLISS VOID YAB-YUM*
AND GRAMMY–NOMINATED MUSICIAN

"Sometimes the modern world can feel overwhelming. Stress and depression run rampant even in the most affluent countries on earth. The good news is that Cory Allen is your new best friend for those times when anxiety has you by the throat. His superhero power is mindfulness. And his ability to break it down in an easily applicable way is second to none."

—DANIELE BOLELLI, AUTHOR OF *NOT AFRAID* AND
HOST OF THE *HISTORY ON FIRE* PODCAST

"Cory will help you think, rethink your thinking, and then transcend your thinking."

—JP SEARS, AUTHOR OF *HOW TO BE ULTRA SPIRITUAL* AND YOUTUBE STAR

T0201596

"We live in a world driven by ego, distraction, and endless anxiety. Learning to untangle ourselves from it is the work of a lifetime, but Cory Allen gives us a surprisingly simple way to begin that process."

—DAMIEN ECHOLS, *NEW YORK TIMES* BESTSELLING AUTHOR OF

LIFE AFTER DEATH

"The journey to Absolute Now is a lifelong calling demanding great courage and persistence. So, understandably, one might need some inspiration. Hopefully *Now Is the Way* will motivate you to stay the course."

—SHINZEN YOUNG, AUTHOR OF *THE SCIENCE OF ENLIGHTENMENT*

NOW
IS
THE
WAY

NOW IS THE WAY

simple mindfulness for modern times

Cory Allen

A TARCHERPERIGEE BOOK

tarcher perigee

an imprint of Penguin Random House LLC
penguinrandomhouse.com

The Library of Congress has catalogued the hardcover edition of this book as follows:

Name: Allen, Cory, author.
Title: Now is the way: an unconventional approach to modern mindfulness / Cory Allen.
Description: New York: TarcherPerigee, [2019] |
Identifiers: LCCN 2019010666| ISBN 9780525538042 (hardback) | ISBN 9780525538059 (ebook)
Subjects: LCSH: Mindfulness (Psychology) | Distraction (Psychology) | BISAC: SELF-HELP / Meditations. | SELF-HELP / Anxieties & Phobias. | SELF-HELP / Personal Growth / Happiness.
Classification: LCC BF637.M56 A45 2019 | DDC 158.1/3—dc23
LC record available at https://lccn.loc.gov/2019010666

ISBN (paperback) 9780593538500

Printed in the United States of America

1st Printing

Book design by Lorie Pagnozzi

Penguin is committed to publishing works of quality and integrity. In that spirit, we are proud to offer this book to our readers; however, the story, the experiences, and the words are the author's alone.

TO MEREDITH

CONTENTS

Introduction

I'm glad that you're reading. It means that you decided to take a moment for yourself. There are no distractions pulling at you. Nowhere you feel like you need to be. Time feels expansive. Your mind is open and ready to soak in what these pages have to offer. You're able to take a deep breath, sink into your body, and engage with this moment of awareness.

Moments like these feel hard to come by. We tend to look at the times we can deeply connect with our lives as a reward. Like me, I'm sure you always have a million things you're trying to stay on top of. The to-do list feels infinite. And that just makes you feel more stressed, which means it will be even harder for you to enjoy a moment for yourself.

It doesn't feel like there are enough quiet spaces in our lives. Distraction is always waiting to pull our attention away and get us fidgeting again. There's never a chance to turn down the stress knob, relax our shoulders, and let our mental chatter go. Living in the modern world, where the input never stops, doesn't help either. Endless digital notifications are lined up, waiting to take a bite out of any moment you have.

But why should feeling the fullness of life be a reward? Shouldn't it just be a way of living? We're taught that we have to suffer now in order to enjoy ourselves later. That just isn't true. It's only one way of thinking. By changing the way we think about living, we can change how we live our lives. The good news is that thinking in a different way isn't hard. In fact, you already know how to do it. You're doing it now. You are here, in the present, focusing on these words.

Think back to the last two beautiful, peaceful, and soulful moments you experienced. Now imagine linking those moments together so they touch end to end. What if we could stretch that moment out? It sounds great. But let's dream bigger. What if it was possible to live in that present, eye-twinkling, connected mindset all the time? Not only is living like that possible, but it has been waiting for you.

THE FULLNESS
of LIFE
SURROUNDS
US.

It only needs us to get out of our momentum of distraction and notice it.

In this book, I'm not going to show you how to simply feel present more often. I'm going to show you how to live in the present. I've spent most of my life looking for ways to feel at peace. I'm sure that you and I are not so different in that way. All of us look for ways to feel content and at ease. In my case, I needed to find a lot of peace because I was holding a lot of suffering. We'll get into what caused some of that suffering later on in the book and how I found my way out of it. For now, I'll tell you that the road I traveled wasn't exactly bump-free. But it worked out well. I'm a happy person and I feel grateful for every day that I spend on Earth.

No matter how frustrated or hopeless I've felt, I always had a small ember of hope in my heart that refused to be extinguished by the cold rain of life. I kept believing, putting one foot in front of the other, and finding my way to more peace. More beauty. More love. More life. I've practiced meditation for twenty years, read every book I could get my hands on, and passed the paintbrush of my mind to Salvador Dalí more times than I can count. All of those things taught me a lot about what it means to be human. However, it was what I started doing next that really opened my heart. I started to listen and allow myself to be the good but flawed person that I am.

Speaking of listening, one of my recent teachers has been my podcast, The Astral Hustle. On my show, I talk to leaders in the fields of mindfulness, neuroscience, and philosophy. It's the greatest form of personal higher education I could imagine. I've had the honor of speaking with people including Sharon Salzberg, Ryan Holiday, Gretchen Rubin, Dr. Dan Siegel, Kevin Kelly, Robert Thurman, Joan Halifax, Dr. Rick Hanson, Matt Haig, Damien Echols, Frank Ostaseski, Dr. Judson Brewer, Donald Hoffman, Lama Tsultrim Allione, Culadasa, Elena Brower, and many others. For an hour a week, I get to ask one of these bright minds how we can make our lives better. After spending hundreds of hours talking with so many incredible people, you could say that I've picked up a few good ways of thinking.

Everything I've mentioned so far will come through in these pages. I'll share what I've learned from my journey and the big ideas that came to me from exploring the minds of some of the most powerful thought leaders alive. I've simmered down all this wisdom into a rich sauce of ideas. This book contains what I believe to be the precise tools to help you live in the present moment, engage fully with your life, focus better, let go of your anxious stress, find balance, and get out of your head and into your heart.

What we'll be focusing on in each part of the book is clear and easy to follow. First, in the "Now" section, you'll learn what the present moment is and how you can experience it, right now. In the next part, "There," we'll take a look at ways we get distracted and pulled out of our lives. From there, we will move to the next part, called "Here." In this section, we'll go over ways that you can bring yourself back to the present, no matter how far away you might be. We'll finish our travels together with a two-part section called "How." This part contains real, actionable steps to help you live a present-minded life as well as my secret playbook of meditation methods.

This book is a fresh take on living better. But the way it's put together isn't what makes it fresh. The way we'll talk is. I want to break the mold on how self-development books typically go. I don't want to serve you thoughts that read well but don't stick. I want your life to change. So, we're going to talk through this book. Think of each small section like we're sitting down for a coffee together. I'm going to share stories and thoughts that honestly helped me in my life. Because I want you to experience real change. I want you to be able to put every part of our conversation to work in your life. I probably don't know you personally. But I don't have to. I care about you. Because you're alive. I know what that feels like because I am, too. I know joy, suffering, pain, and pleasure. I know desire, freedom, hope, and fear. I know what it feels like for your life to start slipping away. And I know how to grab it and pull it back. I want to share all of this with you. Because together in the present moment we can live better, glow brighter, and love deeper. Turn the page, my friend. I'll meet you in the present.

NOW
IS
THE
WAY

NOW

Finding the Present

We say that we want to live better, be present, and feel content. Intuitively, we know that if we get too distracted by the details, we'll miss big parts of the very life we're trying so hard to live. Too often, we look down at our phone, look up, and wonder where the time went. When our head hits the pillow at night, it's hard for us to even remember what happened that day. Maybe if we could be present-minded, we could experience more of our lives. Maybe we could worry less, be more curious, and soak it all in. That sounds like a dream. But how do we get there? What does living in the present moment actually mean? What does it really feel like?

In this opening part, we will discover what the present moment feels and looks like. We won't stop there. I want to create actual change in how you experience every day. So, we are going to go further and get real. We will explore ways for you to turn down the worry knob, build presence into your day, and start feeling the Wow of Now. Right now.

What Is the Present Moment?

Your eyes are closed. Imagine feeling at peace in your body. It's like you've had a heavy backpack on for all of your life and you've finally decided to set it down. Getting used to carrying that kind of weight is easy. It's in our nature to tough things out. This weight hurts your bones, but you are good at carrying on. You're able to make yourself believe that heaviness is a part of life. But today, you realize that you can take off that weighted backpack and leave it behind. When you sling the backpack off your shoulder, it hits the ground with a thud. It thumps the earth so hard you feel an impact tremor run through the ground and tickle your feet. Ah. This absence of weight makes your body feel light. It's easier to breathe and stand up straight. Your spine pops in relief as you relax your shoulders and arch your back. You start to notice a new sensation. The crushing weight of the backpack made you numb. With it off, your body feels like it's expanding and flowing outward in different directions.

The center of your being feels rooted in your heart. Your shoulders and face muscles feel relaxed. A warmth flows into your chest with each breath. Your mind feels calm, crisp, and aware like that of an animal walking through the forest. The tar of bad experiences that have built up inside of you melts away. You feel your feet touching the ground and the ground touching your feet.

You don't feel compelled to grab at the thoughts that are flowing by in your mind. There is no longer a voice inside your head pressuring you to "Go! Go! Go!" and "Get it done yesterday." You're cool. That voice in your head seems to have been charmed by the show of life passing into the windows of your eyes. That striking, beautiful display starts to feel like enough. Life doesn't feel scarce like something you have to grab and hide away in a safe place so no one else can take it from you. It's right there. And there is so much of it.

Then, something else starts to happen as your attention connects with now.

THE **WORLD** FLOWS **LIKE A RIVER** *into* ALL OF YOUR SENSES.

This makes you feel connected to everything. You feel life weaving in and out of you and you begin to understand how you are a part of it. Until now, you always felt like you were moving through life like you were a piece on a game board. Now you feel like you are life itself.

Colors look extra rich. It feels like there's more depth to the space that you move through. Your body ripples from its core with a rising compassion, openness, and understanding. That feeling lifts up and out of you like a warm natural spring.

This is what it's like to live with awareness in the present moment. What you experience flourishes with timelessness. You feel anchored by an awareness of what's happening around you. It doesn't matter if you're standing on the top of a mountain or in the middle of New York City. Everything flows. Natural spontaneity weaves all the parts of life together without effort. A herd of deer running by exudes the same wonder as a cluster of cars coming up the street. Life is connecting with itself and moving along. It's seen everywhere in all things.

Grabbing at Life

The way everything forms around and inside of us is beautiful, but it also presents a challenge. The constant motion of our day creates small thoughts, to-dos, anxieties, desires, and so on. It's like pieces of life bump into us and leave behind a residue. We tend to ignore the pains of life that build up inside of us so we can carry on and get through our day. It doesn't seem like that big of a deal. We think we don't have time to care for ourselves and that we can manage the burden. But when we ignore what we're carrying for too long, our open awareness starts fading. Over time, we get further away from the present until we lose touch with it altogether. Then our momentum shifts back to feeling tense, disconnected, and compulsive. We've put our heavy backpack on again.

When this happens, we stop feeling like we're flowing with our life. We start feeling like we are getting pushed around by everything going on outside of us. This is natural and happens to everyone. Modern life is too complex for our attention not to get lost every now and again. Each of us can count on getting distracted and falling back into bad compulsive living habits. It's only a matter of time. The buzzing sounds and flashing lights of our modern world are too much to ignore.

The entertainment industry creates shows that are designed to make you pause your world and binge on them for hours. Politicians perform media theater in hopes that you'll feel tribal and support them by bickering with an opposing group. Endless marketing campaigns ooze from every pore of our day urging us to buy needless things with a promise of making us feel whole. All of us are addicted to checking our phones every few seconds.

We spend so much of our time dodging the predators of our attention that it's hard to not get tired, lie down, and get eaten. Plus, the whirring of modern life has confused what "downtime" should actually be. Many of us think that sinking deep into our couch and streaming shows for a few hours is a good way to decompress. While that can be fun, it isn't self-care. Nothing internal is resolved when you dive deep into a bunch of episodes. It only provides the illusion of relief. Watching something entertaining shifts our attention away from what's going on with ourselves. When we snap out of the entertainment trance, our attention comes back to reality and everything that was there remains. It's more like leaving the phone off the hook than making a meaningful call.

What's strange is that if you were in the peace of the present and someone asked whether you'd like to end that feeling to check your phone, you'd say no.

WHEN YOUR PERSPECTIVE *is* LARGE, THINGS THAT WERE ONCE **BIG** BECOME SMALL.

You know that checking your phone for the seventy-ninth time that day is a fool's errand. We all know this, but we still do it every day.

It's amazing how fast we can go from feeling calm and present to compulsive, overwhelmed, and freaked out. The mind only needs to

5

make a few small connections before we feel like we're on fire. Over the years I noticed how fast this happened in myself and it made me curious. So, I started paying close attention to how I felt when I went from cool to edgy. I wanted to understand what set off the change in my state of mind, how quickly it came on, and how I could work with it.

When I'm feeling attentive and relaxed, it's like my mind is sitting on a giant pillow inside my head. There is no edginess, pressure, or compulsive momentum. I'm nested *in* the moment instead of being *of* the moment. It's a joy to float through the day and engage each person, task, or thought with my full attention. There's a clarity there that makes reality look like it's in high definition.

Then, out of nowhere, I'll catch myself starting to grab at life instead of receiving it. I could be doing something that isn't stressful at all, like filling a cup with water or making lunch. Then all of a sudden an edginess starts showing up. It's like I have an electrical wire plugged into my body and someone is turning up the voltage a notch at a time. My skin starts feeling like it is sizzling with electricity. The voltage then tries to rise and take over my whole body.

This feeling can show up in such a small, sneaky way. Just enough to make me start feeling like I need to "hurry up" and make my lunch as if I'm late for something. But I'm not late for anything at all. I don't have to talk to anyone for hours. Still, for some reason, my mind starts turning up the voltage. I slowly buy into the illusion. The edgy feeling has an urgency, a pull to it. Like it's trying to draw me in. My mind starts convincing me that if I "get through" these tasks, I'll feel calm and present again.

When you begin sliding away from the present, your brain sends you a message: Get tense, get tight, spin the pinwheel of your mind, and you'll get on the other side of the frantic feeling. But that never happens. It only leads to a racing heart and a fragmented mind. The momentum of grasping gets you balled up in your thoughts and stumbling over yourself. This mindset is the source of much bad decision making. Anxiety takes over and makes you do and say things that aren't really you.

Turning Down Anxiety

We're of two minds: the watching mind and the doing mind. When we're heavy in the watching mind, the present moment comes alive. We aren't processing a bunch of tasks. This makes bonus brain power available to soak in the richness of experience. There are no life equations to solve. We're able to sit back and enjoy the wonder of the answer.

On the other hand, when we get sucked into the doing mind, our brain starts processing tasks as fast as possible. The brain-machine kicks in and analyzes every possible to-do in your mind. It pressures you to "get it all done" so that you can get back to the relaxing "watchful" mind. The problem here is that in modern life, there is no end of things to do. You can spend all day, every day, doing stuff for the rest of your life. We get into momentums of "doing" and they very quickly morph into compulsions. Before we know it, our heart is racing. We become clenched with tension from the stressful idea that we might not be able to get done every task that we imagined. But that's it right there. This anxious cycle of distraction is only an idea.

The sense of presence I described in the opening is the result of a balanced watching *and* doing mind. When your mind is aware and crisp yet calm and seated in the now, you can move through the day without tension. You can indulge in the richness of the present and mindfully do what you need to do.

PRESENCE *is*
PATIENCE.

Sliding into an edgy momentum is what happens when you try to rush past the present moment.

We miss out on the richness of life all the time, in big and small ways. Think of what it's like to take a bite of chocolate while talking to someone on the phone. You put the chocolate in your mouth and chew it quickly so you can get out your important next words. Now imagine being by yourself. You pause and put the chocolate in your mouth. Closing your eyes, you feel the chocolate start to melt. The aroma enters the back of your nose, which opens another dimension of the flavor. Your tongue lights up with the complexity of one of nature's most decadent flavors. If asked, I imagine that we would all pick the second of the two experiences. The difference between them is simple: the presence of mind.

What if much more of your life was lived like mindfully eating that piece of chocolate? It can be. All you have to do is work at it a little each day. Like learning any new skill, you get better at it with more practice. Lucky for you, the modern world is full of things that are trying to steal your attention. You'll never run out of opportunities to work at it.

Start paying attention to when you feel the edgy voltage rising inside of you. The more you watch for it, the sooner you'll catch it each time. When you feel the grasping urgency of your doing mind, remember the thing that's driving the feeling is only an idea. Pause like you're about to indulge in that full taste of chocolate. It's the same thing going on. You're just swapping "receiving chocolate taste" for "releasing edgy feeling." Then let yourself release the idea that is trying to take you out of your presence.

Come back to now. Don't put that backpack on again. Feel the weightlessness. Let your center rise and thrive in your chest. Feel your feet touch the ground.

THERE *is* **ONLY** THIS **MOMENT** *and* *the* **LIFE** MOVING THROUGH **YOU.**

Open and let it move through. Watch and don't grab. Remember that presence is patience. Feel the edgy electricity in your body fade out like a wave crashing and sinking back into the ocean. Be at home in the timelessness of now.

How We Live Between Moments

We don't think about how we go through our day because we're usually busy thinking about what's going to happen next. Most of us get caught up in moving from one thing to another. There is all of this stuff we've decided we have to do and we measure the success of our day by how much of it gets done. There are emails to write, articles to read, posts to like, and of course all the work-life things. Everything becomes a blur. We burn down our wick trying to make the most of the day by getting as much done as we can before we tire out. We're taught that this should feel like a victory. But if we daydream our way through a movie, how much of it did we actually see?

Days slip by all the time without anyone noticing. It's like we open our eyes, blink a few times, and then we're back in bed waiting to fall asleep again. Time seems to blow by while we're keeping busy. This happens because we aren't paying attention. We ride all the stuff of the day like a wave, always balancing on the crest before the crash.

WHEN DO WE EVER STOP *to* FLOAT *and* FEEL *the* DEEP, SLOW MAGIC *of* THE OCEAN?

Not even close to as often as we should. While doing one thing, we plan out the next. We see our life as transitions instead of moments. This state of mind keeps us from experiencing as much as we'd like to think we do. We get stuck in a perpetual state of anticipation.

How much of the time do we think about what we say to people or how we respond to situations? Most of the time we are daydreaming with our attention wrapped up elsewhere. We mindlessly ride the momentum of our reactions and allow our reflexes to call the shots. When is the last time you thought about how you were going to respond in a conversation for more than a second?

Bouncing from thing to thing through the day keeps us living in the spaces between moments. If you live there long enough, the transitions of life get bigger than the actual moments you are trying to land on. This makes life feel as if it's playing in the background like a pianist at a restaurant. It's how we find ourselves in bed at night wondering where the day went.

Think back to when you pictured yourself mindfully eating a piece of chocolate. Now that was a moment. You set everything aside and paused. You stopped thinking about "what's next" and pointed your attention to a single experience. By untangling yourself from the story line of the day, you were able to receive what was happening in a deep way. There was no anxious feeling echoing from within you. No voice trying to make you feel guilty for taking the time to drink life in. You didn't feel pressured to "accomplish" more. You could almost feel a restful, bright, and rooted sense of awareness. You were engaging with what was there. The light of the day swelled and glowed. It was a moment. You released your mind from the details of "what should be" and gave yourself over to the experience of what was.

As wonderful as getting deep into a moment sounds, the space between moments is where we live most of the time. Days often start with a panicked to-do list written across the whiteboard of the mind. Waking hours are then spent rushing to pound that list into submission. We do things almost in an attempt to convince ourselves that the act of doing them gives them meaning. We get excited at the idea of getting ahead on our to-do list. Getting ahead will give us extra time to get distracted by something different!

We spend so much of our lives caught up between places, tasks, and thoughts. We focus most of our attention on our daily mental itinerary and hope it will add up to something big. We think that if we can "get it all done" that we'll be able to find that moment of peace we've been working for. Yet the truth is that you can't get it all done. It just isn't possible. You can put all of your bills on autopay, move into a cabin, and schedule meals for delivery. The mind will still line up a bunch of things for you to organize and deal with.

The brain is a powerful piece of gear. One of its many useful features is to scan our surroundings in search of possibilities. It's a survival thing. Our minds are always seeking to improve, download, and anticipate as much as they can. This helps us stay safe, find food, and make sense of things. That's all great. But the fact that the mind is always assessing everything can get a little overwhelming. Our minds wander freely, try to make sense of the modern world, and then all the static turns into a big cosmic to-do list.

But we don't want to spend our days trying to compute the details swirling through our lives. We want more moments. We want to find a way to be present with our experience and feel each day in a real way. And we can. All we need to do is start aiming our attention in a different direction.

See, up until now, we have let our attention roam free. It bounces from thing to thing and rarely lands on a single experience.

STAYING AWARE *of* OUR PRESENCE *is* HOW WE CAN LOCK INTO *the* DEEP, PENETRATING, RICHNESS *of* LIFE.

Much like we did while eating that piece of chocolate. Of course, the chocolate is only an example. It focuses on an object and the specific sense of taste. But rich moments aren't only to be found in tastes. That's a slice of what's possible. There was a reason the example of mindfully eating the chocolate resonated. It was because we pointed our awareness toward the experience of the taste. Our mind wasn't fragmented and wandering while trying to piece together the details of our day. Our mind was focused, attentive, and fully present with what was happening.

There's no reason to feel intimidated if directing your attention sounds like a hard thing to do. You already do it all the time. Think of the last time you couldn't take your eyes off a thought-provoking film or put down a potent book. Or think back to when you were mesmerized by a musician playing only feet away from you. All of those moments were rich because you had completely focused on them. Your mind was engaged, present, and free from distraction. Finding more of these moments in your life is only a matter of intention. Once you begin living mindfully, everything you experience can be as deep as you want it to be.

Link Your Beautiful Experiences

Little moments of presence have an interesting quality. The more you focus on them, the more they expand. This is why an incredible film can hold your attention for two and a half hours. You don't find yourself feeling the urge to check your phone or daydreaming about what you have to do the next day. You're drawn into the story of the film with your attention fully invested. There's no effort involved. It isn't hard to stay focused on a great story. Quite the opposite, you want to be drawn into it because it's such a pleasurable experience.

This is a key moment for us to make a distinction. There's a reason why this wonderful hypothetical film is so captivating. It's because you are being filled up by the sights, sounds, colors, and emotions the director has woven into a story. You are sitting back, open and focused, receiving the fullness of what the filmmaker has to offer. There is no grabbing at the movie's story or any attempt to control it.

You are allowing. With a present mind, you are engaging with what is happening in front of you.

When our mind slides into fragmented anticipation and our attention gets pulled from the present, it is because we are grasping. We've forgotten to receive life and are once again trying to control it so that our ego feels protected. Caught in a momentum of low-level anxiety, we try to check off every infinite box on our cosmic to-do list.

What if you were able to receive your daily life with as much fullness as you would while watching a great film? You can. Sit back, be patient, and watch. Receive moments in life with the same presence and "nowhere else to be–ness" that you do when you're in a theater. Because really, we don't ever have anywhere else to be in our life except for right here and now. Sure, we do things and go places, but that doesn't mean we aren't there for the experiences. Of course, we are. The difference is how we direct our attention as we take in our own life. Are you thinking about what you need to do tomorrow while you are at dinner tonight? Or are you present with your focus on the meal, the people you're with, and the depth of that wonderful moment?

Paying attention to each moment in life starts shrinking the amount of time you spend living in the space between moments. Retraining where you point your attention might sound hard, but when you give it a try, you'll see how easy it can be. A simple way to start building a command of your awareness is to use one of your pre-existing small routines. Pick something that you enjoy doing each morning. Make a point to pause while you do it, be present, and receive the experience. You're going to be there, spending the time doing whatever it is that you're doing anyway. You might as well engage with it. Drinking your coffee, brushing your teeth, or showering would all be choice moments. Of course, you should pick one that calls to you.

Imagine how your entire day could change if you began each morning by being present for a good moment. Forget making your coffee in a rush and drinking it on the drive to work. Think of how much more connected you would feel if you paused in the morning and shared a moment with your coffee. You could feel the warm, complex flavor roll over your tongue, smooth like exotic silk. As you breathe in the smell and vapor of your coffee, you feel your sense of smell awaken. Your nostrils become warm and open. After a few more sips, you feel the blood vessels in your face and head start to expand. Blood flows and your mind begins to sharpen. Your stomach, now starting to fill with delicious coffee, radiates warmth. Beams of sunlight shine from within you out into the world. And just like that, you turn every morning cup of coffee into a spiritual sunrise.

Experience this deep is waiting for you to receive it every morning. In fact, it's waiting for you to take it in during every moment of your life. All you need to do is break from the daydream of anticipation and release into now.

Choosing a part of your morning routine to pause and share a moment with couldn't be easier. You're already doing the thing. There's nothing to buy, no work to do, and I'm not even asking you to get out of bed earlier. You don't need to do anything different from what you're already doing except focus and receive an experience. What could be simpler?

Something curious happens when you start taking in these little present moments. You build one into your morning. Like drinking your coffee. Soon after that, you begin to see opportunities for other small moments to be present for. You start allowing yourself to receive the feeling of the cool breeze on your skin as you walk outside. Then you find yourself soaking up the glowing warmth that fades in as you spend time with people you love. One day you notice the feeling of each foot touching the ground as you walk. You feel grounded to the earth and your breathing becomes more peaceful.

As these moments of presence show up more and more, you realize that some of them have been touching each other. Actually, a few of them have touched end to end. These long stretches of presence start to fill the day. Then, even more moments start touching each other. Before you know it, the time spent living in the daydream of anxious anticipation becomes what is rare.

Learn from the Old You

Since early on in my life I've found it useful to try to understand how I have changed as a person. I reflect on the pieces of myself that have worn away over time and look for budding growth on the horizon. Looking back helps me see how I'm moving away from old bad habits, damaging personality traits, and echoes of negative life experiences. I also gain insight into positive changes I'm cultivating through my actions and how I can help them bear their transformative fruit.

I was an angry young person. Not in a chaotic way, but in a slow-burning silent way. Quiet types of anger are the tricky ones. At least when someone is explosive, you know what you're dealing with. There are moments that burst and silence between storms. When the anger is quiet, it comes out calculated, cutting, and burning. When I was young, I let the anger out in all of those ways. I felt resentful toward everyone. I wanted to show people, as if they were revealing it to themselves, how smart I thought I was. I always needed to have the mental upper hand.

My family was fractured and I felt out of sync with the rest of the world. There was no one I could relate to except for the great teachers in music and books. Because of that, I idolized musicians, philosophers, and artists as if they were parent-gods. They were the only ones I could trust. Probably because they were the only ones who I thought had anything smart to say.

I was pretty easygoing on the outside, but I enjoyed the art of looking into the back door of someone's mind. I needed to confirm that I was funnier, more creative, and sharper than others were. During this early part of my life, I wasn't trying to become less angry, I was trying to sharpen the samurai sword of my mind. For years, I worked on this so that I could feel protected from any chance of vulnerability.

Slowly, I started catching glimpses of what was under my resentment. The emotional pain of feeling abandoned, loved conditionally, and disciplined by fear was what had been feeding the dark wolf inside of me. The more I began to understand why I was full of so much vinegar, the more the feeling of resentment drained out of me. I could feel it happening as the months passed by. Soon enough, there wasn't any anger left. There was only the pain to work through. That was something I could manage.

Around this time I began paying attention to my mind. I started to understand that if I was aware of how I was operating, I could make choices about who I was. So, brick by brick, I began building the person I knew I could be. Then, an interesting thing started to happen. I felt like I was having huge personal overhauls every few weeks. One by one, nasty personality traits would seem to wear away. I'd pause and think back to how I'd been operating in life only a month before. It was shocking how my intention, patience, and compassion had changed. Skin was shedding.

It was then that I had an insight. I realized that by reflecting on who I was and comparing it to how I felt in the present, I could track my personal growth. This may sound simple and that's because in a lot of ways it is. But for me, contrasting the nuanced changes in my heart and mind took on an important role. I turned those inspiring steps toward love into my new source of fuel.

NO MORE FEEDING OFF *of* FEAR *and* PAIN. IT WAS TIME FOR PEACE *to* BE MY POWER SOURCE.

There were immediate upsides to being nurtured by a positive source of energy. Yes, I was able to use my sense of self-awareness to let go of the negative parts of who I was. But growing a loving awareness also allowed me to move toward new positive things. I was able to gain a sense of where I needed to go so that I could continue to grow. When I reflected on my intentions from a previous month, I could see how I'd let go of more old baggage, delved deeper into my heart, and expanded my point of view. While sober, I'd sometimes feel stoned. The channel of my awareness was opening and the abundance of perspective that rushed in was intoxicating.

Feel the Wow of Now

Only now looking back on that period of my life do I understand what was happening in the big picture. In a rather odd way, due to need instead of desire, I was pointing myself to the present moment. Thinking about who I had been, who I was, and who I could be made me aware of the guy who was thinking about it all.

You can experience a similar sensation right now. Think back to who you were fifteen years ago. Pause for a moment and appreciate how much time has passed between then and now. Picture all the ways your outlook on life is different. How has your understanding of the world changed?

Think about how your body has changed its shape in the past fifteen years. The differences I see in myself are quite clear. I am thinner, healthier, bearded, and rested. My bones are also more rickety and I'm missing the glistening brown hair that once sprung from my scalp.

Don't forget how much culture, technology, and medicine have changed in the past fifteen years, too. During that time, the iPhone, YouTube, and an African American president all came about. It can be dumbfounding to step back and think about how everything is always shifting in one way or another. When enough time goes by, the past starts to feel more like a distant dream than a fading memory.

Let's try to imagine another fifteen-year range, but this time in the other direction. Take the number of your current age and add fifteen to it. I bet that new number makes quite the impact. It sure does for me. But let's take things one step further so that we can feel a new sense of time.

Imagine what your body and outlook will be like in fifteen years. Take the time to stop and picture this with some detail. Use the changes you can see in yourself from fifteen years ago to today as a means to project an equal amount of change forward. What will your face look like? How might new innovations in technology have shaped your life? What will the city you live in be like? How might your perspective on the world be different?

Thinking about yourself in the past and future is a simple way to awaken a new sense of the present. It leaves one with an intoxicating "wow of now" feeling. But that isn't the only way it's useful. I told the brief story earlier to paint a picture of how I stumbled my way into being more present-minded. It was a symptom of my own personal transformation. But let's set aside that flavor of change and consider how observing our growth can be practical.

Pausing to reflect on how often you've engaged with moments in your life is valuable. It's a way to track the progress you've made toward a more mindful approach to living. Everything is always changing, from the edges of the universe to the cells of your body. But change is hard for us to see. The fact that growth happens so slowly allows it to sneak up on us. So, a good way for us to be able to notice a change is to compare different periods of time.

Try taking a break once in a while and thinking about the engaged moments you've experienced in the past months. Do the months that have passed seem like a blur? Or do you recall a collection of grounded moments you've spent on Earth?

These questions yield instructive answers. You could find that you have had a firm hand on the essence of your experience and that you've been living closer to the present more often.

You could also come to realize that you've been caught up in the spaces between the moments. And there's certainly nothing to feel badly about if you have been lost in the grind again. Modern life makes it easy to fall back into living in a momentum of anticipation. It is designed to steal away our attention. This next bit might sound counterintuitive, but it is true: When you realize you are living mindlessly, you are succeeding at living mindfully. Becoming aware that you aren't engaging with the present is the first step of mindfulness.

The path we have traveled in our lives is paved with the mirrored pieces of our transformation. When you look into the reflection of your past, you can see a vital direction for your future.

YOU ARE NOT
ONLY WALKING

YOUR PATH.
YOU *ARE*
YOUR PATH.

How you engage and live in the present moment shapes who you are now. It also shapes who you have the potential to become.

THERE

How We Get Lost

We carry a glowing rectangle in our pocket everywhere we go. Its irresistible shape was designed by the best engineers in the world to feel natural in our hand. Our phones have become an extension of our bodies and minds. We scroll for hours every day hoping to feel connected. But that feeling never comes. This is one of the many ways we get lost in our modern world. Technology isn't the only thing that steals our attention. We even get distracted by ourselves. Did you know that our brains are wired to roam and scan by default?

We're unaware of most of the things that distract us. That's actually what makes attention thieves so effective. They are so good at snagging our attention that we don't realize it's happened until it's too late. Then, there we are, opening one browser window after another as we let our dinner get cold. In this section, we'll take a look at common ways we get pulled from the experience of our lives and how to defend against them.

You're Wired to Get Distracted

Recent research has shown that we have about 40,000 thoughts a day. Let's say you're one of the fortunate souls who gets a good eight hours of sleep a night. That means you're awake for sixteen hours a day. So, 40,000 thoughts a day comes out to about 2,500 thoughts an hour. If you break that down, you'll see that a little over forty thoughts per minute come to your mind. That's almost a thought each second of every waking moment.

Thoughts are like messages that arise in our mind. They appear in the form of words, images, or abstract concepts. Thoughts get a little weird if you think about what's going on with them. Each time a thought arises, it is our brain attempting to make itself realize something. When you think about that last sentence, you get a real sense of the magic of our minds. Because when you read it, your brain was thinking about itself, thinking about itself.

As we just experienced firsthand, thoughts are a fascinating phenomenon. They can carry an immense amount of depth and complexity. This is why they have the power to interrupt our focus thousands of times a day. There's a movie's worth of story layered into each of our thoughts. And as we discovered, there is a fresh one floating through our head almost every second.

With all that activity happening in our minds, it's hard to hold our attention for very long. As you and I know, modern technology doesn't make it any easier to stay on track. I'll be honest. I checked my phone while I was writing the previous three paragraphs. Notifications were coming in and my attention was pulled smoothly over to them. Before I knew it, I was holding my phone and scrolling myself further out of awareness.

Modern neuroscience research suggests that our brain is set to wander by default. Scientists mean this quite literally. The name of our most common brain state is the Default Mode Network. This large-scale brain network is active when we are in states of passive mind-wandering and aren't focused on anything.

Given that we spend the majority of our time in this daydreaming state, it's not so shocking to find out we're wired to stay unfocused. But, there's a good reason why we have such a hard time paying attention more than ever. It's because our biology is far older than our technology. This becomes clear when we roll back the clock a bit and look at our evolution.

Up until about twelve thousand years ago, humans were still hunter-gatherers. During this era, daily life wasn't easy, but it was much simpler. Our ancestors spent large chunks of time foraging for food, hunting, and collecting wild game left behind by predators. There was no reason to cultivate attention because it was only needed in short bursts. The rest of the time could be spent with your mind wandering, thinking about this and that, and watching for threats.

We can adapt fast, but real human evolution takes hundreds of thousands of years. Technology has blown right by us in the race for optimization. Look at it this way:

THERE *are* STILL HUMAN HUNTER-GATHERER TRIBES

LIVING IN *the* AMAZON RAINFOREST, WHILE AMAZON.COM **WILL** DELIVER GROCERIES *to* **YOUR** FRONT **DOOR IN** TWO HOURS.

Technology Is Training You

Our attention is pulled at like never before in the modern world. Let's take a single, universal example: email. Studies have shown that the average person checks their email fifteen times a day. It doesn't seem like that big of a deal. It's only a thumb flick on a phone screen or a quick glance for a notification. There's little physical energy involved. However, thinking like this is what created the illusion in the first place. The disruptive nature of technology is not physical. It is mental. By getting comfortable with checking our email more, over time we are training our mind to be present less.

The overwhelming amount of technology is stealing our ability to have deep, sustained human experiences.

CONSIDER THIS: HOW MENTALLY UNHEALTHY WOULD IT FEEL *for* YOU *to* CHECK YOUR PHYSICAL MAILBOX *the* SAME AMOUNT *of* TIMES YOU CHECK YOUR EMAIL?

To gain a larger perspective, let's move the example on to someone else. Imagine sitting at home on a Saturday and seeing your neighbor open their front door, walk down their driveway, look in their mailbox, do nothing, and walk back inside. Fifteen times. You would find it funny at first. After the third or fourth time, seeing it would get strange and uncomfortable. Ten times in, you might become concerned. Watching them check their mailbox for the fifteenth time in one day might make you want to ask them if they are OK.

This example may seem kind of far out. But the reality is that most of us are doing this every single day. We have a compulsion to break our attention away from our lives. These creeping patterns are so common that it makes it difficult to recognize them as a problem. Don't forget, email is only one example. There are endless things in modern life designed to grab our attention every few minutes.

NOW THAT ADVERTISEMENTS *are* DIGITAL, ATTENTION HAS BECOME *a* NEW CURRENCY.

I'm not against technology. I have an iPhone and an Apple Watch and use them both every day. The issue is that technology is such a powerful stimulant that it is wise to be mindful of how it fits into our lives. We're already wired to be in the Default Mode Network. That makes it hard enough to stay focused as it is. Now that we're neck deep in digital candy, an intentional cultivation of mindfulness has become an important quality to develop. Otherwise, we'll become more distracted at such a pace that we won't notice when we start to miss our entire life.

Getting Stuck in Your Head

Events that are happening in the physical world, outside of our bodies, are not the only things that distract us. In fact, there is a more powerful attention grabber hiding in plain sight. It's us. We have an inner dialogue that's running all the time. This narrative passing through our mind is self-focused for better and for worse.

WE STAY WRAPPED UP IN *the* STORY *of* OUR LIVES, MAKING GUESSES *at* HOW EVERYTHING MIGHT RELATE *to* US.

In most cases, the stories we come up with don't actually involve us at all. We figure out a way to make them connect with ourselves so that we will feel that we have value. The legendary Swiss psychologist Carl Jung defined this natural human behavior as Individuation.

In order for each of us to get a sense of our personal identity, we are always thinking about which traits make us who we are. We compare ourselves to everyone else by looks, wealth, talent, status, psychology, background, behavior, and so on forever. We use the rest of the world and those in it as a mirror to measure our identity. Doing this is natural and useful. It's also a relentless source of distraction.

See, there's not a real healthy limit set on how much we compare ourselves to everything else. Our minds often spin out into complicated stories that keep us distracted for long stretches of time. We get stuck in mental loops. Through the lens of imagination, we decide how others see us, how we behaved in the past, and what the future holds.

Think of the last time you went out with friends, got home, and spent hours worrying about something you said. Remember all the scenarios your mind threw at you before the last important meeting. One that's too common is feeling like you look worse than everyone else in a photo with bad lighting. There are countless ways we get snared in comparing ourselves to the rest of the world. It's rarely useful, but we do it all the time out of a compulsive need to gauge our imaginary value and remain self-focused.

When you combine everything that pops up in the world and in your mind, you come away with a ton of distractions. Constant digital nudges, environment scanning, and self-comparison come with another cost, too: stress. Having our mind churn away while it tries to keep up with all the pressure of modern life creates a huge cognitive load. Carrying the weight of this stress wears us down. It makes us tired and even more vulnerable to distraction. No wonder everyone has so much trouble staying connected to the present moment. We're up against a lot nowadays.

Having realistic expectations about your ability to stay focused is important. None of us should assume that we will reach a point where our attention is unbreakable. We should also make sure not to beat ourselves up if we get sucked into a period of mindless living. As we touched on earlier, our brains are wired to scan for information. Getting distracted by our thoughts is a natural and involuntary process. It's similar to when we get stressed and our breathing becomes unpleasantly shallow. Both of these bodily functions turn on by themselves. But that doesn't mean we can't change their shape when we notice them.

Every so often, I would assume on a more tense day than usual, you will notice that your breathing is fast and shallow. You know this isn't good because short breaths and a tight chest are signs that you're stressed. So almost automatically, you pause, take a deep breath, and fill your lungs with air. You might even let out a deep sigh when you exhale. The response to realizing when your breath is short was built over time. You made the connection one day that the more stressed out you got, the more you felt like you were suffocating. To help ease the problem, you figured out that taking a long, deep breath was revitalizing. This is, of course, a useful response for anyone to build into their behavior.

But notice that you don't get self-critical when you realize you're breathing has become shallow. You recognize what's happening and rely on a mindful response to adjust your breath. Working with the command of our attention should be no different. Being present-minded isn't a competition. It is a joyful pursuit. Just because you get stressed sometimes and start breathing fast doesn't mean you are bad at breathing. The circumstances of life lined up in a way that made you feel too pressured and your body had a reaction. Our mindful attention works the same way. Sometimes your attention will fade out of the present and you'll find yourself rummaging through your thoughts. It's no big deal. It just means that it's time for an adjustment.

When you notice your train of thought has slipped back into a momentum of anticipation, try to treat it like you would shallow breathing. Pause as you catch a glimpse of your distracted mind. Like taking a deep breath, pull your attention away from the distraction. In the same way that you would let out a deep exhale, point your focus at something specific and engage with it. Focus strong and sharp like a hawk. You could lock your eyes on an object, taste something, listen to the sound around you, or draw a fresh, bold thought to the front of your mind.

Breaking out of distraction by placing your attention on a single thing is a useful way to reclaim your focus. Just the same as you would reclaim your breath. With a little practice, resetting your focus becomes second nature.

Breaking Free from Thought Loops

While reclaiming our day-to-day focus can become easy, breaking free from thought loops can prove to be more of a challenge. Extreme mental states can make us obsessive. A jolt of fear, excitement, confusion, or stress can narrow our awareness with ease.

Think of the last time you felt anxious about something and, even with logic on your side, couldn't let it pass. This is a thought loop. It is when the mind spins up with an idea and you can't get it out of your head. The thought has gained momentum like laundry circling around in a washing machine.

When you find yourself caught in a thought loop, it is often because your emotions peaked too fast. A feeling jolted you, your mind began spinning, and you are having a hard time slowing it back down. In these situations, it's quite difficult to point your attention elsewhere. So, how can we slow down the spinning thought? You'll have a hard time letting go of a thought that's causing a negative obsession. It's spinning with too much speed and has too powerful of a momentum. You need to introduce other thoughts into your mind. Start a conversation with a friend, get up and go for a walk, read a book, or do your grocery shopping. Engage with other things that force you to tend to them. Dilute the obsessive thought. Sure, it takes time to slow down the spinning thought loop. But by adding other lines to the story in your mind, you can transition to another mental state. Gently, you can find your way back to the peace of the present.

You Are Not Your Thoughts

Life evolves from circumstance. What we experience is a series of situations. We do one thing and that leads us to the next. Although it is seamless, most of what happens in our lives comes together by chance. Let's say you found a lucky "heads-up" penny while you were walking down the sidewalk. That's a lighthearted and fun momentary feeling that happened by chance. There was no plan that brought this experience into your life. At no point did you call up a friend and ask them to leave a heads-up penny at a specific location and time for you to "stumble upon." You found it by chance. That's what made it lucky and exciting.

Much of life works like the lucky penny. All the parts of the world follow their own little narratives as they unfold through time. There are so many story lines going on that they can't help but bump into each other. Randomness serves each of us exhilarating wins, deflating losses, and a lot in between. But this chance woven through our daily walk is a big part of what gives life its magic. We never know what could happen next. And that's what makes us want to keep following our story and watching for that next lucky moment.

The mystery of chance isn't only out in the world. It's also in our mind. The random thoughts that pass through our minds can lead us down all sorts of interesting paths. Think of how many times you made what felt like a basic choice that ended up leading to the unexpected. There is a potential for surprise waiting in everything. Even in the thoughts that arise in our mind.

And this brings up a valuable point.

YOU *are* NOT YOUR THOUGHTS. YOU ARE *the* THOUGHTS YOU TURN INTO ACTION.

Each of us has an endless supply of thoughts that form in our mind, which then move along and disappear. Remember, we have a new thought almost every second of the day, so there is plenty to go around. Each of the thoughts that form, whether good or bad, comes with a certain amount of potential. A large part of mindful living is being able to recognize thoughts as they appear and respond to them, not react. Responding and reacting might sound similar, but there is an important difference: When you react to your thoughts, your actions are based on reflexes. When you respond to your thoughts, you are self-aware and able to act in a mindful way.

INTENTIONALLY CHOOSING *the* THOUGHTS YOU DECIDE *to* TURN INTO ACTIONS *is* WHAT BUILDS WHO YOU ARE.

Inside the privacy of your mind, you'll get stuck on a negative thought sooner or later. We all do many times a day. But, if you engage with the present, you can recognize that thought as negative and choose not to express it. This is a simple and powerful way to reduce suffering. By letting that negative thought pass, you kept yourself from expressing it to the world.

This means that the only place the negative thought existed for a short time was in the privacy of your mind. You then allowed it to evaporate and move on. When you chose not to turn the negative thought into action, it kept the negativity from becoming part of who you are. This allows the reflexive snarky comment, defensive verbal jab, or unfair judgment to move by without hurting anyone.

Being mindful and aware of how we express our thoughts also gives us the power of potential. If we can face the chance of our day with a present mind, we're less likely to get into situations with negative potential. When we are aware of the thoughts that are arising, we are prepared for almost anything. It enables us to be patient, make compassionate choices, and reduce the suffering in our lives.

One of the ways that we get lost in a momentum of distraction is by getting pushed around by what is going on in our life. Each of us feels like we have a bit more than we can handle showing up on our plate each day. The stress of making sure we do what we need to do to make our lives happen can be draining and make us frantic. What if we have so many meetings at work that we have to eat lunch walking from one meeting to the next? What if we're stuck in traffic when we're supposed to be meeting our partner for a special dinner? Life happens, but we can set up for success by building things into our day that help us stay engaged with what is before us.

Giving some sort of shape to your day makes a remarkable difference in how you feel. Even though this is a simple thing, building a gentle daily structure is something that many people miss out on. It isn't their fault for missing it. They are simply too overwhelmed by the frenzy of their grind to have the space to think about anything else. And that is what adding shape to your days will give you. Space. Breathing room. Steady rocks to step on as you walk across the bubbling river.

A Daily Routine Will Keep You Focused

You can start simple. And actually, I hope that you've already begun. Think back to earlier when we touched on finding an experience each morning to fully engage with. A mindful, patient pause to actually taste your coffee. Feel its warmth. Breathe in its vapors. Doing this gives your attention a morning wake-up call. It is a simple and joyful way to start each day with a reminder that another morning is a gift. This mindfulness ritual is the first part of giving shape to your day.

There is an endless number of things you can add to your daily routine to give it the shape that serves you best. I don't look at these things as chores. I look at them as gifts that I give myself. I know that if I follow my routine, I will feel my best, stay present-minded, and make my most valuable contribution. It took some exploring, but over time, I found the combination of activities that give my day the strongest frame.

Having a present mind is one of my top priorities. I came to intimately understand that the way we experience reality is based on our mental state. Knowing this makes me sure to keep my mind well supported so that I can be as positive a force in the world as possible.

I like running. I'm tall and have long legs, so I'm designed for it. Running has a timeless, meditative feeling to me. It's like instant mindfulness. You have to pay attention to where each foot lands or else you're bound to fall. Been there. The repetitive nature of planting one foot after another is peaceful and hypnotic. Feeling the system of your toes, ankles, knees, and hips working together is a constant lesson in balance. Plus, you can't do anything else while you are on a run. Running demands your full attention. There's no chance you'll get sucked into sorting through emails or zone out while thumbing at your phone. You're there, breathing, sweating, feeling alive. And nothing else.

I run first thing in the morning. Then, after getting cleaned up, I mindfully drink my coffee and eat breakfast. I down my mineral and B-vitamin capsules with a green superfood mix. Then I meditate. I've been meditating for about twenty years. It is, without question, the most important tool in my life. (I look forward to sharing more with you about that in later chapters.) After my morning meditation, I start in on a project that needs work that day. I have lunch a few hours later and always eat the same thing. A smoothie bowl. It's kind of a thick fruit-and-greens smoothie poured into a bowl with crushed cashews and granola thrown on top. After that, I have an espresso and get back to work until the evening time. I also make it a priority to get a full night's sleep. If we do not rest well, we do not recover.

AN UNRESTORED BODY *is a* LIMITED ONE.

These are the nonnegotiable parts of my daily routine. They can expand and contract, but they must happen. Each one I described serves a specific function that contributes to my clarity of mind. Running wakes up my body, gets my blood flowing, and works out the primal animal need to move. Drinking a single cup of high-quality coffee gives me a caffeine boost that crisps up my mental speed. The vitamins, minerals, and green superfood ensure that my body has plenty of the fundamental nutrition it needs. That keeps my energy sustained and hunger in balance.

Meditation, as I mentioned before, is the most powerful force in my routine. When I meditate, my body and mind are given the time to relax, expand, and ground. Meditation tethers my heart to now. My lunch gives me another dose of essential nutrition. It's light so that it doesn't weigh me down. It's only what I need to get another energy boost and keep the fire burning. You'll notice that the caffeine that I have after my lunch smoothie is not another cup of coffee. It is an espresso. I intentionally reduce my caffeine intake during the afternoon. Doing this gives me another little mental boost, but keeps me from getting the coffee jitters. Caffeine overload is a surefire way to fry your mind and raise your anxiety.

Any restorative moment that you can make a habitual part of your day will serve you well. Even if it's only a tiny blip. Take one minute to sit, breathe, and let go before you walk into the building where you work. Stretch for a minute or two after you get out of bed. Check in with yourself while you are in a conversation to make sure your body is relaxed and open. One of my favorites is to pause, only seconds, before each meal to make sure I eat slowly, with respect and intent.

All of these simple things I've turned into a routine may seem small. But they are responsible for giving my days a powerful shape. The extra 30 percent mindfulness boost they provide is unmistakable. I rely on it to make the best of myself come forward. Caring for yourself is crucial. It breathes extra life into your decision making, creativity, awareness, and compassion.

I keep the effects of what I say and do in the front of my mind as much as I can. Of course, I'm far from perfect. Without thinking, I say things that come out wrong. But I truly do my best to pay attention to what I put out there. What we choose to say and do can have impactful, long-lasting effects, much larger than we realize. For better and for worse.

A dear friend of mine told me recently that something I said years ago had stuck with him. The insight I mentioned to him changed his perspective and helped him live with less anxiety. When he recited what I'd said to him, I didn't even remember saying it. This was a good lesson for me. It taught me that even the things we forget that seem small to us can be big to someone else. After he shared this story with me, I felt grateful, knowing that I had been present with him in a moment when he needed my attention.

Lasting positive impacts like this are why giving my day shape is so important to me. One small choice, a singular and brief conversation that memory forgot, has the potential to create authentic change.

The chance of life is not in our favor. It isn't against us. But it isn't on our side either. It only *is*. We can't create our luck, but we can do much to change our effect. As we pass through the randomness of life, we will encounter more situations, conversations, and moments than we can imagine. We can be present-minded for each of those moments. And then, our response to what we meet will be aware, compassionate, and give way to the greatest potential for positive effect on our fellow humans.

Giving shape to your day will help you weave threads of compassion through the fabric of time. Establishing routine self-care allows the opportunity for the best you to show up. The you that is engaged with each moment. The you that is drinking life in. The you that is compassionate, loving, and patient. The you that is there for the people around you and doesn't even recall being helpful.

MAKE YOUR CLARITY *a* PRIORITY *and* EVERYTHING WILL CHANGE.

You will understand yourself, your life, and those around you with openness and ease. Love will visit your heart more often. We indeed cannot control the dips and turns, rises and falls, of our life. But by living mindfully, we can vaccinate ourselves against chaos.

You Balance Your Mind When You Balance Your Life
It's alluring to go far in one direction. Deep diving into one aspect of our life gives us a sense of purpose. It firms up a part of our identity and relieves some of the pressure that each of us feels to find our role. While it can be healthy and exciting to jump headfirst into a dimension of life, it can come with a limiting effect. When you have the light of your focus shining on a single thing, your life outside of that light is in darkness.

Often, we will intentionally wrap ourselves up in a juicy part of our personal narrative. There's a comfort in knowing what you will be chewing on every day. Trimming down your identity also comes with a sense of control. It gives the people in your life system limited ways to think of you. If our passion becomes imbalanced, it can turn into blinders. A narrow view can keep us distracted. This can get tricky. As our aim gets more centered, we start ignoring other parts of our lives without realizing it.

Boxing ourselves in can keep us feeling comfortable. However, as you build your sanctuary, you also build your jail. Many people find their personal sanctuary in their professional lives. It can be hard not to in the modern world. It is reinforced that to be a successful person you've got to rise above others, and we usually do that by buying into an illusion of our choice. But people find their distraction in all kinds of things. Of course, it's not only good but crucial to have passions that you're giving yourself to. It stokes the fire of the soul. What is key is that life is in balance.

WHEN LIFE GETS
TOO FAR
OUT *of*
BALANCE,
WE FALL.

And when you fall, you get hurt.

I became obsessed with music in my early teens. I'm being literal when I use the word *obsessed*. A genuine compulsion for music had swept inside of me. For years, there was hardly a moment when I didn't have something playing. Even at school I would put a Discman (keep in mind it was the '90s) in a backpack to have with me. I'd keep the Discman playing in my backpack and run the wire from a pair of earbuds under my shirt and out of my collar. Since I had long hair in those days, I could sneak the earbuds into my ears and put my hair over them so no one could see. This let me listen to music all day, even during my classes. At home, I'd take breaks from listening to music to learn to play instruments and write my own songs.

After finishing high school, I worked in record stores and eventually started my own music production company. During those formative years, I would go to my job, come home, and work compulsively on my own music until I fell asleep with my head on my desk. After an hour or two of sleep, I would go back to work, come home, and do it all over again. I skipped almost every social invitation or opportunity for a good time. I had a razor-thin focus and besides reading or meditation, music was all I could do. This went on for years. I have no idea how I managed to survive on such little sleep or how that fire burned with such a high level of fury for so long. There was a lot of good that came out of those years. By spending countless hours in my music laboratory, I was able to become a self-taught professional music producer. I also released a lot of records. All of it was a crucial first step in what became my weirdly evolving professional life.

THERE

But hindsight often offers a much clearer version of the truth. Looking back, I can see that what was bordering on a clinical obsession with awakening my musical consciousness was also a form of denial. I'd turned off as many lights as I could in my reality so the things I didn't want to face could hide in the darkness. And staying distracted by the one remaining light came with its fair share of negative effects.

I was unhealthy. Sleep was for the weak, I thought. So, I slept for an hour or two a night and drank my weight in coffee. In all seriousness, I took one-minute naps during the day to keep going. I'd fantasize about falling forward limply, letting my body smack the ground flat, and passing out. The hilariousness of those kinds of thoughts was another way to get by. The whiskey river flowed. I drank every night to numb my aching body. That approach didn't exactly encourage a healthy emotional well-being. And Nietzsche's collected works were on my side. I used his writings to arm myself with the belief that emotions, like sleep, were signs of weakness.

The calcification of my emotions left me socially ignorant, defensive, and arrogant. This all was unfolding while I was steeped in the teachings of Buddhism, too. As some do, I was missing a large part of the point and using Zen to become more clinical and detached. Truly, it took meeting the woman who became my wife to learn how to build a bridge out of that pit. I saw that Zen does not seek detachment, because doing so will leave you grasping at nothing.

BEING
EMOTIONLESS
IS STILL AN
EMOTIONAL
STATE.

The mind has a way of hiding our pain from us so that we can carry on. In extreme cases, it is a valuable feature. If you could acutely feel the pain of having a root canal when you recalled the memory of having one, you might never go to the dentist again. Life would be too tragic if our minds didn't bury the pain among our memories. We may not feel the pain from the moment of our bad experiences, but we can feel the dead grass above where they are buried. Who could blame us for wanting to add some extra dirt on top of that spot?

Although tempting, adding dirt on top of our buried painful memories so we can get lost in distraction resolves nothing. It makes things worse. The parts of ourselves that we shut down lose the ability to see. Through this form of mindless living, we become numb to our own life as it passes us by.

When your life is in balance, so is your mind. In order to stay charged by the muse of your own vitality, it is important not to ignore any part of yourself. When you allow your professional life, relationships, self-care, and passions to have space, there will always be room for you to breathe. If you can breathe, then you can sit deep in yourself and feel grounded. You can be present-minded and engage with the moment. You can be there for your life as it scrolls by.

Take Small Steps to the Present

As I've gotten older, I've come to learn that showing up for each moment is one of the most meaningful things we can do.

BEING PRESENT *for* THOSE BREATHS, LAUGHS, *and* SMILES IS THE ESSENCE *of* LIVING.

You can let go of all the edgy anticipation and stop trying to live five seconds in the future. When you do, eyes light up and deepen like they are their own singular universes. Muscles of the body soften, find a restful peace, and fidgetiness fades. This is when the heart begins to open. The warm expansion of quiet love is able to rise from you like steam from a teacup. Then you can be there to share the moment with the people you care about and let the joyful conversation flow. And it flows.

FINDING OUR BALANCE *is* WHAT HELPS US FIND OURSELVES.

But our outer life is not the only place that should concern us. We should seek to balance our inner life. The first foot that falls on the path of self-discovery is met with a strike of excitement. The invigoration moves upward into the heart, through the body, and finally, to the mind.

When you figure out that it's possible to become more awakened, it's like discovering that you have superpowers. And you do.

YOU HAVE
the POWER *to*
SHAPE WHO
YOU ARE.

Through self-reflection, you can understand yourself from the outside. This is why it is called *self-reflection*. Looking inward is like looking at yourself, your mind, and your intention in a mirror. This kind of reflection can help you understand yourself more deeply. Awakening to fresh understandings of yourself is the foundation of change.

Once you see your inner self from the outside, you are able to recognize your own behaviors, thought patterns, and perspectives. Many of them will not look as you hoped. But this is why self-transformation is exciting. It's why I called it the "muse of your own vitality" earlier. By seeing yourself more clearly, with honesty, you are able to spot the parts of yourself that need to change. You can see what parts of you are holding back other parts that are dying to thrive. Then, with that self-awareness, you can choose to do something about it.

Self-realizations come in every shape and size imaginable. Since they are insights, they are thoughts. And thoughts are what construct our reality. Say one day you're having lunch with a friend and you notice that you have a habit of talking over them each time you feel their sentence winding down. You are eager to jump in and contribute more to the conversation. There's no intention to be rude. In fact, it's the opposite. You're so excited that you're bursting with words. But by rarely letting your friend finish what they are saying, it comes off as if you don't care what is being said. After you spot your behavior, you then notice how your friend becomes more deflated with each interruption. So, you make sure to be more patient and mindful before you speak. By choosing to turn your insight into action, you have changed and brought more of your best self forward.

That was a small, nuanced change in self. It dealt with a negative trait that is common among many people. But as I mentioned earlier, self-realizations come in all sizes. Years back I got into an odd habit of visualizing myself from the outside. At first, it was like I had an imaginary camera ten feet above me at all times that played in my mind's eye. Then the view zoomed out. I walked around with an aerial image of my city in my mind. My precise location in the city moved like the blue location dot on Google Maps. Then the imaginary camera view in my mind zoomed out even further. An image of our planet Earth, from a great distance, found its place in my mind.

I could never escape the imaginative view of a lonely Earth floating in space. The notion that I was somehow stuck to the blue spinning spaceship of a rock stayed with me, too. The absurdity of this image etched in my head made me laugh. Until the image shifted again. The image of Earth in my mind disappeared and there was only me floating in the middle of infinity. The thought of floating there in our solar system began giving me anxiety. Mainly because it was true. We are, indeed, all floating in space and my awareness of it had become acute.

My heightened awareness of being a cosmic castaway left me stunned by the infinite nature of our universe. That jail of thought gave me great anxiety as to what meaning, being, and truth actually were. This state, which lasted a few years, is what I refer to as my existential paralysis. I wrestled with being and my search for meaning often gave me pause. Eventually, I found my way out by moving from my head to my body. Running and yoga are wonderful antidotes to thought quicksand.

Each time we make ourselves a little better than we were before, it feels like a victory. That's because it is. We have reprogrammed the programmer. Finding balance in our inner growth makes our path smooth and fluid. I shared the story of my mental "going out of bounds" as an example of how being unbalanced in your pursuits can lead to struggle, suffering, and another kind of distraction from the present. Sure, I came out of my existential paralysis with lengthy notions about meaning and truth. But the experience was filled with suffering. It was also yet another way to ignore parts of myself that needed addressing.

Personal wisdom can come in large chunks, but most of the time it is best served as small bites. That's because we don't ever have to stop changing. The refinements can and—I feel safe in saying this—should continue over the entire course of life. We can keep watching and making little adjustments to ourselves. They add up to big things. If we follow the trail of bread crumbs and patiently eat one at a time, our development will be stable and well integrated. It also helps us avoid getting bloated from the delicacies of the bakery.

HERE

How We Get Back

We've learned how we get distracted, feel anxious, and miss out on big parts of our life. This is important. Understanding a problem is the first step to solving it. I hope you've been able to identify at least a few key things in your day that are eating up your attention. Now that we have a good idea of what's getting us lost, we can look at how to find our way back.

In this part, we'll explore helpful methods to get us in touch with the present moment again. From suggestions about positively rewiring the way we think to how we can stop worrying about our to-do list, this part is packed with useful ways to feel more present. There's even a breathing exercise that will light up your senses! Alright, my friend, let's go fill our cup with the richness of life and drink it down.

Why We Miss What's Right in Front of Us

Simple things are easy to miss. And we miss them. What's interesting is that we don't overlook what appears obvious because we don't notice it. We overlook what seems obvious because our mind thinks of it as "known." You and I are designed to operate in this way. See, our brains have only so much energy. When they decide they have the full picture of something, they move on. The brain ignores what is apparent because it has evolved to constantly scan its environment. Our lives are spent with darting eyes. We are not looking for what is there, but for what is new or different. What is "there" then fades into the background as we look to the horizon.

Think of how easily you get used to sensations. Only when a sensation is interrupted does your attention draw back for another look. Let's say you decided to go on a dream vacation: a safari in Africa to see some of Earth's most beautiful animals in their natural environment. You sit parked in the touring car. As you look out across the field of tall blonde grass you hope for a glimpse of an incredible lion.

While you wait, you admire the grass itself. The blonde grass is long, full, and strangely uniform in height. The wind moves through it in a sensual way. Each strand of grass responds to the wind on its own, but is mysteriously connected in a wave of motion, breathing with its siblings. The movement hypnotizes. Suddenly, you notice a distinguished lion has teleported only a few dozen yards away. He is crouched down, using the line of the grass as a disguise. When the wind blows, his powerful blonde mane blends with the waves of grass and he seems to disappear. You keep your hopeful eyes locked on the spot where you last saw the lion resting. You wait for a glimpse of the enchanting creature as he moves. The sensual blonde grass fades.

We are always looking for the next thing. The modern world teaches us that happiness is obtained. It should be something we can hold and show others. If our happiness is heavy and weighs us down, then that will prove it has value. We are taught to grab at life and take what is ours. Then wear it around for others to see. This way of thinking is ingrained in us all but leaves our hearts wanting. Together, we walk around like excited Labradors, waiting for a treat from the world that it can never reward. But that feeling often makes us go harder, want deeper, and lean further into looking for what is next. The final answer must be right around the corner. It feels close.

Our intuition stirs at this moment for a reason. The answer is indeed close. But we keep looking just past it. The way is not forward. The way is now. The peace, fulfillment, and home that we all look to grasp, to discover, with such earnest heart is here.

The ABUNDANCE *of the* PRESENT MOMENT *is*

WAITING FOR US *to* STOP LOOKING FOR WHAT *is* NEXT *so* THAT WE CAN SEE IT AGAIN.

We have become used to what seems obvious and have stopped looking. Now has faded out like the sensual blonde grass in the Sahara. Our gaze is strong in the direction that we last saw the lion's striking, delicate mane. We are caught, hoping for a glimpse of what we have been told we must grasp. The lion is our desire.

When we get too wrapped up in grabbing at what we think will make us complete, we stop being able to see what is apparent. The anxiety of wanting makes the abundance of what is already here blurred and faded. Desire is not only in things. We desire to hurry up, feel in control, be perfect, make others more like us, and so on. We miss the beautiful blonde grass in the hope of spotting a lion. The edginess of wanting keeps us clenched, blind, and distracted from the moment.

Life is happening all around us. All we have to do is allow ourselves to slow down and take it in. But it's tough to go against our design. And the complexity of modern living makes it even harder. We feel that we almost want or need to be distracted all the time. Distraction has the illusion of comfort. Take a look around any public place or even your living room, and you'll see the tops of heads, eyes sunk into glass screens. This kind of addiction to distraction, which comes in too many forms, draws us out of the present. When sucked into a phone, we scroll the glass screen with a finger and the world scrolls by our bodies. There is such an allure to giving our minds over to the computer, phone, or momentum of fidgety tasks. Because our minds are spinning, we feel like we are getting somewhere. This feeling of the hunt draws us in. All the while, our bodies tense and harden. Managing the urgency of anxious distraction adds to our stress, turns our back muscles into a curved shield, and limits our senses.

Experiencing the present moment is simple. You are doing it right now. How deeply you are engaged with it is a question of another sort. See, it is not what you do to become more present, but what you don't do. At first, this will feel counterintuitive to your ego. Up until now, we—you, me, everyone—have been taught that we should fill the space before us. We have been told that we have to build more structures, fill our homes with more things, and "do more." Our society commands us to stay busy if we want to look productive and be perceived as valuable.

Hoarding objects and thoughts has proven, time and time again, to lead to more suffering. So let's try a different approach. Instead of adding things, thoughts, and tasks to our day, how about we go in the other direction. Let's try removing things. With greater empty space in our minds, there will be a clearer view from the windows of our eyes. With more empty space in our bodies, there will be more room to breathe.

Let's Experience Now, Right Now

I'd like for us to do a short experiment. I want you to get a taste of what it is like to engage more deeply with the present moment. The change you notice during this brief adventure will be small and nuanced. But think of it like an arrow pointing to a larger potential. Know that we will walk down that path later in our journey together.

Read the instructions and then actually do what they ask. Picturing it in your mind won't have the same effect. You have got to experience it firsthand to understand what it is. Think of the difference between hearing how a delicious meal tastes versus tasting the food for yourself. The experience is beyond words. Stuff only the mind and body can absorb through a direct connection.

I know it can feel odd to follow instructions from a book. It can make you feel self-conscious, embarrassed, or kind of silly. Do me a favor and let that go as much as you can. Take a few minutes and give yourself over to this small observation-based experiment. At the very least, it will make you feel more grounded. It could also give you an insight into what engaging with total presence is like. Not just a single object, such as your morning coffee.

Step 1.

First, let's do some research on your current mindset. After you're done reading this step, I want you to look up from the page and do what I describe. Take a good look around the space that you're in. Make sure to notice the edges of the objects that surround you. Absorb the colors you see. Look at how the light is landing across space and the way shadows are cast. Feel the distance of everything around you.

Now, I want you to get into your body. Feel the tension in your shoulders and how the muscles in your face stretch. Put your awareness in your arms and legs. What are they resting on and how are they positioned? Can you feel the areas of your body that are supporting your weight? Does your body feel heavy?

Finally, I want you to listen. Really open up your ears and see how much you can draw in. Are some sounds close to you and others far away? Is it apparent that sounds are happening in front, behind, and to the left and right of you?

Now that you have paused and taken in your moment, I'd like to move on to the next step.

Step 2.

This step is active and where it really counts. And it's good to go all in on this one because it's fun, and at the very least will brighten your day. One last time, I ask that you perform these instructions, as opposed to only reading them. Otherwise, you won't feel any of the effects. And I want you to feel it because it feels great.

We are going to do a simple kind of breathing exercise. Make sure that you're sitting on a chair, couch, or bed. You can also lie down if that feels more comfortable. There are two reasons for this: One is that I want you to be able to relax. The other is that I don't want you to be standing on the off chance that you get a little light-headed.

Sit or lie down. Allow your arms and legs to go completely soft. They don't have to be unnaturally limp like noodles, but they should be relaxed.

Close your eyes. Take ten long and slow deep breaths. Raise and expand your chest on the inhales and let your chest fall on the exhales. Then, take twenty rapid short breaths. Channel your inner panting dog. Then take ten more long and slow deep breaths. Finish with another twenty rapid short breaths. If you feel hungry for more, do another ten slow and twenty fast. Open your eyes.

Step 3.

Welcome back. Now, we are going to do mindset research like we did in step 1. Take a look around you. Remember, the change is subtle but see if anything is different. Does the space you're in have a different sense to it? Are the colors and light that you see brighter? How does the distance of all the objects around you feel? More open?

Check back in with your body. Has the tension in your face and shoulders relaxed? Do your arms and legs feel like they are resting without effort? Does your body still feel heavy, or does it feel light, almost as if you're floating?

Listen once again to the sounds that surround you. Do you have a more detailed sense of what and how many things you are hearing right now?

That concludes our experiment. I hope that you did the breathing exercise and felt a shift in your perception. Although it is simple, the new sensations that can be felt by following the steps above highlight something that until now we had only been talking about. It's the arrow pointing to larger potential.

I wanted you to do that breathing practice because it serves several functions. Taking slow and deep breaths calms the body and focuses the mind. Taking rapid breaths lowers the carbon dioxide in your system, which makes you feel a dash of intoxication. When you put these two back-to-back, you come away with an interesting effect. Your calm mind recognizes the intoxicated feeling and cuts through it with its heightened focus in order to stabilize. This allows you to have a momentary heightened sense of awareness. Another reason for this practice is to get you to sit, if only for a few moments, and focus on a single thing: your breath.

This experiment offered a taste of increased awareness. As you direct your attention to the present moment more often, that feeling of crisp and spacious presence will begin to appear frequently in your life.

AWARENESS
GROWS.

And with it comes the gift of sitting deep in your body, free from a momentum of anticipation. You'll then notice that you are grasping at life less, opening up, and receiving more. One day, you will wonder why you were ever grasping at all. There was never a reason to. And you will not only know this, but you will feel it. You will be able to rest in it. Because you'll know through feeling that we are being held in the caring hands of our own existence.

We are set free by appreciating the sensual blonde grass. There is nothing to gain from ignoring it in order to look for the lion's delicate mane. When a lion appears, there it will be, and we will soak in its tremendous glory. Then the lion will pass. And we will not grab at its memory and become anxious with a desire to see it again. We will go back to admiring the sensual blonde waving grass until we meet the lion once more.

We Adapt to Our Surroundings

It's incredible how quickly we are able to adapt. You can put a person in unimaginable situations and the mind and body will change as necessary in order to survive. Take a rather extreme example, like a physical response to starvation. The moment our body recognizes we haven't eaten for an alarming period of time, a massive chemical shift happens inside us. Through no conscious effort, our biological resources are optimized. Going with no food feels awful at first. We become irritable, our head pounds, and we are weak. But then, our body helps out once more by configuring itself to the new normal. That makes us feel stable again. If you've ever fasted, you know what I'm talking about. There is a period of discomfort, but after a short time, you break through the haze and your energy returns.

All things considered, starvation is an uncommon case of human adaptation, one that I hope you don't ever experience. But extreme examples aside, we are adapting all the time in small ways. Every day, we shift who we are to mesh with our surroundings. When you spend time with your friends, you speak freely, honestly, and with shared slang. While people are at work, they often become more reserved and speak in a controlled and guarded way. During family visits, certain topics are avoided and there are many nods to past bonding moments.

We change how we speak, what part of ourselves we want to share, and our references to a culture based on where we are and who we're talking to. This is a form of adaptation. Behavior is altered, ever so slightly, so that we can shift our colors like a chameleon. We are trying to match our environment. It is a nuanced shift, but it happens with almost every interaction we have. That's why spending time with some people feels so great. They match up with us in a way that allows the best part of who we are to come forward and thrive. These are the people you want to be around. As we will find, they help shape you into the person you want to be.

Sometimes people change how they portray themselves based on their surroundings. To me, it is interesting to watch the kind of enchanting, ritualistic effect that a space can have on people. A while back, I stayed at The Standard hotel in downtown Los Angeles. Their rooftop bar is a nightlife destination that has a lovely panoramic view of the city.

One evening we decided to head up to the rooftop bar, have a drink, and soak in the view of Los Angeles. The bar was a scene, packed tight with people who were determined to have a good time. But that wasn't what interested me. I prefer low-key situations. What caught my attention was the entrance door to the bar. I watched, with childlike wonder, people melt into someone else as they crossed the threshold. While on the pathway leading up to the bar entrance, their walk was stiff, their movements were awkward. As they passed through the door, their shoulders swooped, their stride became smooth, and they rose with confidence. It was a mystical doorway indeed. With true fascination, I watched each person shed their skin and adapt to the idea of what it meant to have a good time.

Behavioral changes like these are simple reflections. We mirror who we are talking to or where we are for the moment of the experience. It is how we connect and figure out a way to respond to the world. But if you look deeper, you will find that we can use this mirroring part of our nature to make real changes that last.

Rewire Your Brain for Peace

There is a great deal of scientific research showing that our brain can rewire itself. This ability is called *neuroplasticity*. Our brain is home to about a hundred billion neurons. These neurons are special nerve cells that can send signals. When we have a thought, the different zones of our brain work together. Neurons communicate by sending signals across the bridges that connect them. These bridges are called synapses. When signal patterns in the brain repeat, our synapses strengthen.

I like to think of brain synapses as roads. Every time we start a thought, the neurons in our brain send signals down these roads. This process connects the areas of the brain and completes the thought. When we think in repeated ways, these roads become more developed. With enough repetition, they can develop from gravel roads to highways. These brain highways allow signals to move through with more ease. It also encourages similar brain activity to use the established path. Who wouldn't want to take the highway instead of a bumpy gravel road?

So we can, and do, create lasting change in our brains. Think back to the first time you drove a car. Chances are high that you were nervous and the ride wasn't so smooth. You hadn't become used to working the pedals, turning the wheel, and watching the road all at once. You had to learn how to be gentle, use the right amount of pressure, and anticipate the movement of other cars. After a few weeks of practice, you became more comfortable behind the wheel. And when you drive now, you show up at your destination without thinking about how you got there.

Our brain pathways become smoother as we develop new skills. They are bumpy at first, but through repetition, they become second nature. Mindful living not only changes our habits but our actual ways of thinking.

BEING PRESENT GIVES US *a* GREATER AWARENESS *of* OUR DECISION MAKING.

When we are engaged with life, we have the power to choose what thoughts turn into actions, and which actions turn into habits.

By engaging with the moment, we can rewire ourselves to think in more positive ways. What's interesting is that we can actually choose to be more loving, patient, and open. We can also decide to let go of negative thoughts that create suffering. Mindfully curating your behavior starts changing the infrastructure of your mind. As brain roadways change for the better, it becomes instinctive to be kind to others and to receive life fully.

When we live in the present and choose compassion, all the pathways of our mind start changing shape. Highways of compassion and awareness become the thoroughfares of our brain. Good habits develop. We respond to life with warmth.

And remember, our occasional critical or judgmental thoughts enjoy using the highways, too. It's a faster way to travel. When the main roads in our brain are paved with positivity, all the thoughts that pass by absorb the good vibes. Through repeated mindful decisions, we can change our entire outlook on life. New thoughts arise into a positive framework. Being giving and warmhearted becomes a reflex. The world starts to gleam with optimism and potential. The roadways of negativity go unused and begin to unwire. Then they fall apart.

You Can Break the Mold

During the first two dozen years of my life, I felt like I was always on guard. I had a self-protective need to be prickly. People who spoke to me would be offered a verbal jab, a cynical word to take them down a notch, or a foul joke to make them as uncomfortable as I was. The pain and resentment I was holding made me feel fragile inside. I needed armor and a defense mechanism to keep people from getting too close to my hidden raw nerves. When a dog barks and bares its teeth, it is not an antagonistic gesture; it is a defense. The animal is displaying aggression to keep you back. Active defense. That was how I found comfort in the world.

Even though I had a way to keep the world back, it didn't mean that I was free. My suffering had been packed in crates and dropped to the bottom of the ocean inside of me. The way I saw the world was clouded with negativity and cynicism. The crates were leaking. And the negative worldview was not only a response to my suffering but a form of distraction. Judging everyone I saw, criticizing people I knew, and belittling emotions was a way to stay numb to what I needed to feel. It was a cynic's script carved in stone.

Pressure builds up when you pack away your feelings. No matter how rock solid you are, the pressure gets to a point where it finds its way out. The more you fight it, the more unpleasant a path it will find to escape. We are like teapots. When we fill with steam, we start to squeal and need to release. Somewhere in my teens, I discovered meditation. It was like a medicine that I could take in the privacy of my mind. I found that no matter what was happening out there, on the inside I could start to change. I realized my inner life was mine and that in my mind I had freedom. The choice to heal was available. I simply needed to make it.

I meditated every day. At first, I only felt flashes of peace. Maybe calling it peace is too generous. It was more like finally being able to rest. As I went further, some of the crates packed with my suffering that had sunk to the bottom of the ocean began to rise. They peeked out of the surface of the water and floated in waiting. My continued meditation practice allowed me to be present enough to look inside the crates. Then I could start to acknowledge what was inside. It was then that real transformation became possible.

Several years passed and I remained dedicated to meditation. I kept my practice private and kept working with my crates. I knew that if I changed myself on the inside, my growth would be apparent to everyone else. One day to my surprise, my growth became clear to me. I realized that I wasn't responding to as many things in life with active defensiveness. I was more accepting and not as quick to judge. My reflex was no longer cynicism. It was hope. Hope that my feeling of rest could transform into one of peace. I'd become an optimist.

Meditation was my entry point to the present. The increasing awareness of what was going on right then, in that moment, allowed me to understand what I was thinking and feeling as it arose. My presence helped me engage with what was coming up. From there, I was able to choose. I could decide, in the moment, to let go of the negative thoughts that came into my mind. There was no need to express them toward others and cause harm. They could simply pass through my mind and be forgotten. By engaging with the moment I was able to get on the other side of my conditioned responses. No longer was I flinging sour words as a reflex. I could feel the tug inside, a dare from the dark wolf in my soul, to say something nasty. And chose not to.

Firsthand, I watched the sun rise in my view of the world. The darkness of my cynical, negative mindset was illuminated with positivity and compassion. I had rewired my brain. Meditation showed me how to live mindfully. My awareness was pushed further into the present until I was able to gain freedom from my negative mindset and choose to live a better life.

To watch my point of view go through such change showed me that we all have an incredible potential within us.

BY LIVING IN *the* PRESENT MOMENT WE WILL BE MORE AWARE *of* OUR **THOUGHTS** *and* ACTIONS. THAT GIVES US *the* POWER *to* CHOOSE.

When we are dedicated to choosing good, our view of the world changes. It grows into the shape of peace. And so do our lives.

How to Practice Being Present

I'm sure it would be easy for you to come up with a list of things that you do every day. Maybe you stretch after you wake up, grab a coffee after lunch, or meditate before bed. We do these things for a reason. They make our life better. We've learned from experience that if we do a handful of small things each day, they'll add up. These behaviors are habits. We tend to have a negative association with the word *habit*. That's because there are helpful and harmful habits. People have a tendency to look past what they are doing right and focus on what they wish they could be doing better. So, the idea of intentionally creating new habits feels a little counterintuitive. Create new habits? Like start smoking?

But we can create helpful habits in our lives. What's interesting is that when we repeat a behavior for long enough, only a few months, it becomes ingrained in us. Again, kind of like a reflex. So, here's a different way to think about this. If new habits form into behaviors after a few months, we can continue shaping our behavior as much as we'd like. When the habit we introduced a few weeks ago is becoming solid, we can add a fresh one. And repeat.

WE CAN LITERALLY BUILD OURSELVES INTO *a* PYRAMID *of* OPTIMAL BEHAVIOR.

I've found habit-forming to be a useful method for increasing my mindful awareness. All you need to do is pick one small thought. Then associate it with a behavior and put it in the back of your mind. It's like writing a word on your hand so you won't forget a larger idea. And if you want to do that, it would work, too. But for now, let's stick to working in our mind. There is so much going on in our lives that it is incredibly easy to get distracted. We forget about things we were passionate about only hours, or minutes, earlier. So, by attaching a mindful thought to a behavior, we can set a reminder for ourselves. And as we touched on earlier, these behaviors become ingrained over time and add up big.

There are countless moments in the day when you are "on hold" as a person. Little moments of space where you are paused while waiting to do something else. Things like waiting in line, riding in an elevator, commuting by train, or idling at a traffic signal. These brief universal human moments are ripe for habituation. One day I spotted these on-hold moments and it kind of blew me away that I hadn't noticed these empty spaces before. From then on, I started making use of those moments. When I find myself in one of the on-hold moments, I check in with my body. I relax my shoulders, correct my posture, and take long deep breaths. It took some effort to remember to do that at first. Now I do it without even thinking about it. It's become a habit that is like a quick hit of mindfulness.

Another time in life when you can build mindful habits is during conversations. Communication is our greatest gift as a species. It is what sets us apart from the other animals on the planet. In fact, our complex speaking ability is why we survived and Neanderthals did not. Our language is filled with so much nuance, rhythm, and perspective that there are endless opportunities to use it to build mindful habits.

There are many layers to speech. The words coming out of someone's mouth are one thing, but the idea they are trying to express is another. When someone is talking, they are usually doing a fair amount of improvisation. They have a general idea about what they are trying to express, but they are also figuring it out as they talk. That's one of the fascinating ways that we understand ourselves. We have a pool of ideas right under the surface of our awareness. But to get a good look at them, we've got to talk them out into the atmosphere. Because of that, people usually express their idea in chunks. They need to get a few words out, pause to think about what they've said, then continue trying to piece their idea together.

Let me share a habit that I've enjoyed building while in conversation. I like not only listening to the words someone says, but to the idea that is running underneath the words. It's a unique way to get a deeper understanding of what someone is trying to communicate to you. It takes patience. And that's part of the mindfulness practice. Conversations are exciting. The resonance of two minds opens a channel of thoughts that neither of you has had before. When both people dedicate themselves to the conversation, an incredible energy builds. The excitement of a good talk makes it hard not to cut in, talk over someone, or talk for too long. I've found great reward in being present, patient, and attentive to the ideas while I'm engaged in an exchange. Next time you're in a good chat, try fully giving yourself to it. Don't spend time thinking about what you want to say next. Be there and respond rhythmically. Notice when your attention drifts and pull it back to the person you're engaged with. Open up your body language. When you unfold your limbs, expand your breath, and relax your shoulders, the depth of your words will flow more freely. Give good eye contact to show that you're interested. Each of these things will make you a better conversationalist and thinker.

Being present in conversation clarifies your thoughts and speech. This is because your mind isn't simply wandering while you wait for your turn to talk. You are actually present, in the moment, and paying attention.

WHEN YOU ARE
MINDFUL IN
CONVERSATIONS,
YOUR VERBAL
GLITCHES
WILL FALL
AWAY *and* YOUR
SELF-EXPRESSION

WILL SHARPEN.
And THAT SHARPENS
YOUR ENTIRE LIFE.

Set Mindful Reminders

Negative thoughts are the seeds of negative actions. The occasional criticism, judgment, or bit of negative self-talk is bound to pass through your mind. And if you've ever felt bad for having a foul thought about yourself or someone else—please, let yourself off the hook. Every person who's ever lived has had their share of harmful thoughts. These passing negative thoughts aren't even important. What we do with them is. I assure you, one of the most life-changing mindful habits you'll ever make is letting go of negative thoughts.

Countless feelings and ideas come up as we experience each moment. I look at these arising mental formations like pathways. Every thought is an opportunity to shape the moment that will come next. Much of the time, we are surprised by what we find ourselves saying and doing. This is because we are distracted and not engaged with the present. Our thoughts turn into actions in a reflexive way. But, if you are mindful of now, you will be more aware of the way you exist in the world.

Try slowing down how quickly you respond to what comes up in your mind. The speed of the modern world bullies us into compulsive action. Once you step out of the momentum of hectic living, you will see it is only a suggestion. Not a necessity. Be patient.

THERE IS NO
RUSH *to* BEING.

Start paying attention to the thoughts you are having. Watch how you respond to them. When a negative thought arises, the ego often urges us to spit it out as fast as we can. The ego tries to trick us into believing that by demeaning others we will have more value, or be more secure. Of course, this isn't true. The only thing expressing negative thoughts does is create more suffering for everyone.

So, you can build the helpful habit of being present with your thoughts at the moment you have them. When a negative one comes, you will be able to see it coming and choose not to express it. You can let go of negativity. When a mindful awareness of your thoughts forms as a habit, you will begin to have fewer negative thoughts. Of course, there is a distinction to be made. Don't confuse negative thoughts with justifiable negative emotions. The negative thoughts I want you to let flow by are the unfair judgments and criticisms of yourself and others. On the other hand, legitimate grievances that cause negative emotions are important and should be addressed. Confronting what makes you feel negative is how you can create positive change in your life. Habits like these will rewire your brain and change your outlook on the world.

You can attach mindful reminders to any kind of feeling. Even challenging ones. All you need to do is make a mental association with them. Then practice it a few times, until it turns into a habit. I'm sure you feel little flashes of stress, frustration, or irritation that pop up now and again. Everyone does. These overwhelming moments don't feel good, and they never will. But we can associate these feelings with a behavior that helps us recover from them faster. Try looking at these short bursts of feelings like alarms. Each lightning strike of stress, frustration, or irritation can act as an alarm bell.

When you feel them ding, let the urgent bad feeling become the alarm that reminds you to come back into the present. You can build in a response to these feelings that instantly begins to disarm them. When your shoulders clench and your neck tightens, respond with a deep exhale and inhale. Stretch your body a little. Loosen up. Shake off the negative reflex. It helps. Once this habit forms, decompression becomes the natural next step after tension.

Don't give up on building mindful habits if you have a hard time remembering to be present. There are ways to give yourself a helping hand throughout the day. Years ago, a dear friend of mine was working toward his doctorate degree in molecular biology. I don't know how much you know about that world, but it isn't pretty. During these years my friend slept for only a few hours a night. He was hardly able to eat, and when he did, it was usually fast food. He had to work long hours in a laboratory in the hope of getting good experimental results. If he got good results, he had to write a monstrous technical paper about them. Then, if he got that far, he had to defend his paper or spend his nights writing grant proposals.

The science life was exciting for him at first. As the years wore on, the extreme stress and lack of sleep became a grind. Then it became torture. We would meet up each week and I would do my best to listen to what he was going through. I offered as much encouragement as I could. He started losing his hearing and having equilibrium problems because of the stress. He was getting paler by the day. I could tell he was breaking apart. One day, while staring off into the middle distance, he said, "You know, I guess people really do go crazy." That was when I knew things had become serious. He was so swept up in a tornado of stress that he couldn't even catch his breath. And he'd been a practicing Buddhist for more than a decade!

So, at that moment, I tried to think of something I could offer him. Some way to ground him amid the chaos that didn't rely on him having to remember to do so. And luckily, I thought of something useful. I suggested that he put a reminder on his phone calendar titled "BREATHE" that went off every hour. That way, no matter where his head was, he felt an hourly nudge in his pocket that reminded him to come back to the present. For one minute each hour, he could step out of the tornado, take some deep breaths, and ground himself.

There are ways to give yourself a hand if you have a hard time remembering to be present. It could be a written note that says "Now is the way" or a reminder on your phone. Do what works for you. If you discover that you don't respond to one method, try a new one. Try to have fun with the creativity of it. Play around. Eventually, you will find a way to build a foundation for positive habits in your life. After that, anything is possible.

Ditch the Infinite To-Do List

Zoom out a few clicks. Think about all the stuff that's going on in the world. Pause and consider how many things are happening right now. Birds are flying by. The grass is soaking up water from the soil. Ants are rebuilding their freshly disturbed mound. Someone is in their car on their way to a job interview. They're tingling with excitement and nerves. Another person is waking up on their wedding day. They wonder what emotions will rise and if everything will go smoothly. A scientist sits in a laboratory and contributes to research that will one day cure cancer. Emails shoot into inboxes. Volcanoes rumble. Coffees are made. Wine is poured. Pilots fly a tube filled with hundreds of people across the globe. Your tissue cells regenerate. You exhale.

There seems to be an infinite number of things happening all around us. Right now. And always. By the magic of nature, it all works and stays stuck together. I've always been struck by the idea of infinity. Of course, the standard definition of **infinity** is "something that has no limit." But I also like to think of "personal infinity." This is when there is a limit to something, yet it is too great for us to grasp mentally. That doesn't make the thing infinite, but it makes it infinite to us. For example, if you think in terms of personal infinity, there are an infinite number of people. No matter who you are, Obama or the Dalai Lama, it isn't possible to meet all seven and a half billion people on the planet. So, even though it isn't literal, there is an infinite number of people out there based on what you can experience. This is a fun idea to toy with, but for now, I want to aim it at our lives.

The number of things that happen around you in each moment is infinite. There are always more emails to write, pictures to post, work to do, and cleaning to be done. We have so much coming at us all day that it's hard not to feel overwhelmed. Plus, the modern world has added a certain pressure to it all. Sure, it's a gift to be able to email ten people, in ten countries, in ten minutes. But the speed available for us to communicate with other people has backfired. Since we can send fast, we are expected to respond fast. A new kind of social pressure has been born. We feel obligated to stay wrapped up in the frenzy of the digital age. If we don't, we fear that we could legitimately hurt someone's feelings, or simply be left behind.

I kind of love stumbling upon digital oddities. I often leave my phone in a room that I'm not in for hours at a time. Every once in a while, I'll pick up my phone and find that someone has played out an entire text conversation by themselves. They will even resolve disagreements with themselves. I'll pick up my phone and find five or ten texts from the same person. The first one is a question. The second is a nudge about that question. Then, about thirty minutes later, they text their view on the question. And finally, they tell me they've figured out their initial question. Then they ask what I'm up to. It amazes me when I find these completed scripts. They are like diamonds forged from the intense pressure of our digital age.

One way or another, our behavior is changed by the pressure of modern living. We each exist in a personal ecosystem of social pressure, pop-ups, and to-dos. When will it end? It won't. It can't, actually. All these bits need to keep coming so that life can keep unfolding. While this is true, it doesn't mean we are destined to be battered by notifications for the rest of our life.

There's a certain suction to the infinite to-do list. I feel like it taps into our survival mechanisms. We're wired to eat, protect ourselves, and find a tribe. These aren't things that we want to do. We have to do them. It is our nature. The urge to do them will always pull at us in one form or another. For hundreds of thousands of years, we have had to locate our water, gather our food, and find a safe place to rest each day. Our human reward for doing these earthly tasks is a feeling of wholeness. We know we have squared our survival for the day. We are able to rest.

Cure Your Evolutionary Hangover

Times have changed, but we haven't. Not that much, anyway. We are still struggling to integrate ourselves with the rapid advancements of technology. I call this growing pain the *evolutionary hangover*. The pressures of the past have been replaced by new ones. But a large part of our mind is still operating in ancient ways. We still feel that important need to square our survival for the day. Now that we're living in a modern tech era, our daily tasks have grown to be infinite. Responding to email is the new finding our water. Liking social media posts is the new gathering our food.

The issue is not that we've changed how we live, but that we are now surrounded by infinite options. They are overwhelming. And we feel a need to get it all done. Whatever it is. We're driven to respond to every email, like every post, and watch every video because deep down, we are trying to square our survival for the day. But we can't get it all done.

WE NEED *to* LEARN *to* MANAGE OUR PERSONAL INFINITY.

If we don't, we will get sucked further out of awareness. That is not where we want to be. Because a distracted mind never finds its place to rest.

My mind tries to pull my attention away from the present all the time. It actually makes me laugh. These bubbling distractions are so creative and persistent that I almost admire them. When I sit down to do the simplest thing, even something I want to do like reading a book, my mind always offers a few alternatives. Maybe I get hit with a sudden urge to follow up on an email or read the Wikipedia page about the book I picked up. Although, these distractions don't arise as offers. They appear as to-dos.

IMPORTANCE *is* *the* DISGUISE THAT DISTRACTIONS LOVE *to* WEAR.

Getting derailed by thoughts keeps us from engaging in the present moment. When we are distracted, we are thinking about everything except what is in front of us. How can we overcome the barrage of distracting thoughts and pressures of modern living?

First things first. Let's address the suction of the infinite to-do list. There is a reason we are in a trance of compulsively responding to our notification-filled lives. Living that way came on gradually enough for us to think it is normal. And when we think something is normal, it seems like the only way. There's also a fear that if we pull away from the digital suction, our lives will change for the worse. We worry that friends will get upset and we'll miss out on opportunities. We worry about being out of sight and out of mind. They are understandable fears to have. Luckily, none of them are true.

To take control of your life, you'll have to choose to change. Set firm boundaries. The urge to check your email in the middle of the night or glance at social media one more time are only impulses. And I have good news for you.

YOU HAVE WILL OVER YOUR IMPULSES.

Think of it like a diet for your mind. What happens when you're trying to cut back on calories and get an urge to eat a cookie? You discipline yourself because you know that you'll feel better in the long run. The urge to eat a cookie rises and you pause. You recognize the impulse, dismiss it, and continue on. The urge is a trick of the mind. You've spotted it for what it is and not been fooled.

Pulling away from the river of digital suction works in the same way. Allow yourself the space to take a few steps back from it. Pause, breathe deep, and let the impulse to engage with Internet chatter pass. Trust yourself. Gradually, the urge to "get it all done" will fall away. Don't be too hard on yourself if you get snagged by it again. It happens. Think of it like cracking and eating a big slice of cake while you're watching your calories. Recognize you slipped up, learn from it, and keep letting one breath lead into the next. Soon, the new normal will be life without the feeling of a constant urge to square your survival for the day. The feeling of completion will show up more often. And you'll be able to rest.

How to Deal with Distracting Thoughts

Now, let's work with the constant rise of distracting thoughts. Our mind is designed to scan and compute. The issue is that it never stops. The thinking switch is stuck in the ON position. That is because we are alive. You are happening, right now, as a person. For that to continue, everything about us needs to keep pumping, breathing, and thinking. So, when we try to pause on one idea and focus, our mind keeps offering more thoughts. Really, our mind is trying to help us by offering up an endless stream of ideas. It wants us to be well prepared and have plenty to work with. It also wants us to stay wrapped up in the drama of our own story.

I've found a good way to keep from getting distracted by my random thoughts. Let's say I'm about to write an email. I have the browser open, the text box is up, and the cursor is blinking. I know what I need to say. The moment before I strike the keyboard, right as I'm about to release my energy into typing, I'm hit with a mental nudge. It's like a billboard lights up in my forehead. The image in my mind is an urgent one. I must change the song I'm listening to. Right now. Of course, I don't need to change the song and it doesn't matter. But my mind tries hard to convince me that it is important and urgent. I've learned, however, not to be fooled by my wandering mind.

When a thought interrupts my focus, I acknowledge it. This may seem like I'm allowing myself to be distracted. But I'm not. By acknowledging the thought quickly, I recognize it. I see it for what it is. I recognize it as a distraction, which keeps my attention from being lured away. Then I let the distracting thought go. Actually, that could be too gentle a description for what I do. Letting a thought go

is the process of releasing it so it can melt back into nothingness. When I'm actively doing something and I have distracting thoughts,
I like to give them a little boost. After I recognize the interruption,
I give the thought a mental push. I bat it away like the thought is a
tennis ball and my focus is a racquet. This could sound strange, but
give it a try. The next time you are interrupted by a thought, pause
and recognize it for what it is. Then visualize the thought getting
knocked out of your head by a firm forehand.

Write Out Your Flow

A tough time to stay present is when we feel pressured by a mountain
of work, errands, and emails. Having much to do with little time to
do it can be stressful. It really gets the mind going. This is because
your mind has picked up the pace. It's revving up like an engine so
that it can peel out when it hits the gas. This is good when you've got
a lot to do. You can find yourself in a flow state of focus, accomplish-
ing one thing, then the next. That is if you don't blow out your engine
first. See, when our mind revs up to get ready for a busy day, it isn't
only the focus part of the mind that's charging. The whole thing is
getting worked up and that includes our distracting thoughts.

I'm sure you've noticed when you're stressed, your mind is extra-
active with distractions. That's because your thought production is
higher than usual. Of course, this means your interrupting thoughts
are coming faster, too. When I find myself in a state of mind like
this, my mind gets crafty. It uses my to-dos as a form of distraction.
As I focus, a rushing series of thought billboards appears. They
try to distract me by applying more pressure. How will I get this all

done today? Is it even possible? Do I have enough energy? What will happen if I don't get to everything?

This type of distraction is common when we're feeling extra pressure. It can be overwhelming because it's adding fire to the flame. Our minds can only hold so much at once. We panic when we know we are overloaded. Imagine if I asked you to remember two numbers. Easy. But what if I asked you to remember six numbers? It would be a little harder, but I bet you could do it. Now, what if I asked you to remember thirty different numbers? It'd be too much and feel overwhelming.

When I'm feeling distracted by the pressure of a stressful time, I immediately do one thing. I get organized. I write out everything I need to get done, from most to least important. That way, I can keep track of where I am and address what is most crucial. Doing this relieves the pressure of distraction because you're no longer in danger of forgetting something. You've cut off your mind's anxious fuel supply. Interrupting thoughts become quiet. You're able to stay in the present and calmly focus on one thing at a time. An amazing thing happens next. You realize the whirlpool of stress was all a daydream. And you get into your flow.

Honesty Will Keep You Present

It takes the same amount of energy to say honest words as it does to say false ones. Yet, we aren't honest all the time. We can't be. There are too many moments in life where softening the truth is actually a compassionate thing to do. Say your partner suggests going to their favorite restaurant. When asked, you might say, "That sounds good," even though it doesn't. You know that going to your partner's favorite spot will make them happy. So you soften the truth for them. Of course, softening the truth can scale from a simple dinner reservation to complex moral questions. You and I would agree, in many of these situations, that total honesty isn't always the highest moral choice. Especially in situations where there are no foreseeable negative consequences.

Dr. Brad Blanton developed a self-help technique that takes any form of lying, no matter how innocent, off the table. It is called Radical Honesty. And it sounds pretty dangerous to me. The method suggests that a person should offer their unfiltered honesty at all times. Regardless of how rude or hurtful it may be. The general idea is that doing this will reduce the stress that one holds and lead to a clearer way of living. Author A. J. Jacobs gave Radical Honesty a shot and wrote about it in his book *The Guinea Pig Diaries*. To put it mildly, he did not discover that telling the total truth at all times was an effective way to reduce his stress. Telling the whole truth put him in one uncomfortable situation after another. He ended up being mean. Some people found his sharing with them to be disturbing. Especially since he was being totally honest for no real reason at all—other than to not soften his internal dialogue of truth.

I won't be trying out Radical Honesty anytime soon. To me, it sounds closer to a social disorder than it does to self-help. I love Larry David's character on *Curb Your Enthusiasm*, but I wouldn't want to be around him in real life. I think most well-adjusted human beings know when it is sensible to withhold a dash of honesty. Maybe not in every nuance of daily life, but at least when it counts. Moments like those are somehow apparent. You can feel it in your body like a magnetic charge. It's like the universe is pushing on you, urging you to choose the poetry of the heart over the math of the mind.

When I was twenty, my phone rang a few days before Christmas. The caller ID—keep in mind this was 2002—showed that the call was from my father. This came as a surprise. My father had not been in my life since I was a small child. I expected a short phone call each year and hoped for the occasional visit. For him to call during the day on a day that didn't seem significant was a shock. Excited, I picked up the phone. But it wasn't my father. It was his wife's family calling me from his home. My father had a medical emergency and was at the hospital where he was to have open heart surgery. He was in a coma by the time my brother and I got to the Dallas–Fort Worth area from Austin. We never had a chance to speak with him. He swelled up with fluid because his organs were failing. The puffiness made him look like an adult-sized baby, helpless, leaving the world looking the same way as he had entered. My eyes saw hyperreality while his hung open and unfocused. The heart monitor beeped like a metronome of life. Time, the movement of blood flow in cycles, somehow kept him in his body.

My brother and I waited several days in the intensive care unit. We listened to the extended family of our father's wife, whom we had never met before, condescend to us. I peacefully shielded myself from their ideological aggression with the pages of a book by Julian Jaynes. After endless surgical meddling, my father's heartbeat crashed and they had no choice but to give him CPR. That pushed the blood clots in his heart into his bloodstream. They then traveled to his brain, where they did irreparable damage. It was the end. On

Christmas Day, we let our father and the machines that were keeping him alive finally rest.

Sadly, this tragic event only interrupted a different, longer one. Leading up to the end of that year, the health of my father's mother had been declining rapidly. She had been suffering from Alzheimer's disease for some time. When she first started getting confused, it was uncomfortable but bearable. I would ask her if she was hungry and she would tell me no. I would worry that she was indeed hungry but could not remember to tell me. So, I would go ask her a second time. She would say she was fine and that a sweet boy with brown hair had just asked her. Eventually, her mental state declined to a degree to where she couldn't recognize anyone at all. Not even her two sons.

After my father died, I remember there being discussion around whether to tell my grandmother her son had passed away. She was in hospice care and clearly close to her own end. She would call my uncle by my father's name after he was already gone. I remember, so clearly, chewing on this question then.

What is right? Radical honesty? Should we try to convince a mother who can remember nothing, who is weeks away from dying, that she had a son and that he died? Wouldn't that only confuse her further and add to her suffering? Was it unfair to keep the knowledge from her? What if there was a sliver of awareness under her veil of confusion that wanted the truth?

These are questions that have no correct answers. They can only be met with personal judgment. I remember getting a clear answer when I ran these questions through my twenty-year-old mind. There was nothing to ponder. No logical arguments to make. I felt what was right. It was apparent. The feeling replaced the marrow of my bones. And it was then that I had an insight that has only solidified with time.

HONESTY *is*
WEIGHTLESS.

How we decide to engage with it is the weight we must carry.

The way we choose to live our lives shapes who we become. If we go against the feeling in our bones of what is right, then we will carry the weight of our choice to do so. I certainly soften the truth to be compassionate and keep from being rude. But I don't lie. I'm honest with the people in my life and with myself. Because, I have learned that when you are honest, you are light. Remember, honesty is weightless. The opposite is not. Being honest removes the stress, fear, and drama from your life. It keeps your mind clear and your heart open. You have nothing to carry. You are light. That is how you fly.

It isn't possible to be in the present when your mind is full of dishonest stress. You are always anxious that the truth is lurking. Worried that your story will fall apart. The anxious momentum of dishonesty will keep you distracted. Flashing memories of past dishonesty pull you out of your experience. The dread of what might come out will always be on the horizon like a dark cloud cover. Peace cannot be found in a life of dishonesty. These types of distracting thoughts make you miss the beautiful life that is right in front of you.

To stay here, in the abundance of now, we must practice honesty. I use the phrase "practice honesty" for a reason. This is because being honest or dishonest is a simple choice. You can go anywhere you want in this life and be honest the whole way. The modern world sometimes suggests to us that it is normal and even necessary to be dishonest. Especially when we are competing with others. But this just isn't true. Think of the extra room you'll have in your brain from not worrying about being dishonest. Imagine the energy you'll have to devote to what you love if you aren't drained from the stress of bad memories. Honesty gives you energy. It gives you more room for peace, creativity, and love.

Telling the brutal truth is not a way to stay in the present. It lacks compassion and creates unnecessary suffering in the world. Being dishonest is also not the way. Doing so causes stress to build and leaves you dragging the weight of your worry. The way of presence is the way of choice. When you decide to live a life of honesty, you become weightless. You float. You expand. You glow. Vitality charges. Most important, you are free. Free from the burden of your mind. Free to experience the vast essence of the present. Your mind is clean without worry. Your heart opens without fear. The mind and heart expand and touch. You are here.

HOW

How to Live in the Present

Here we are. We know what the present moment is, how to feel it, and how to find it. We've seen the ways that modern life, the grind of getting through a day, and even our own mind can pull us away from the joy of living. If we do get caught up in the buzzing of being and get lost, we've discovered how to find our way back to the present. Now it's time for us to learn how to stay in the present.

The final part is where we'll take all the ideas that we've soaked up throughout the book and put them into action. We're going to take them forward with us into the future. We're going to feel a real change and live better. "How" is split into two sections. One is to be done in the world. The other is to be done in you.

The first one is called 12 Ways to Now. It is a collection of twelve guiding principles. You don't have to act on them all at once and you shouldn't. They won't grow into you that way. Look at these twelve ways like a playbook for life. Think about them. Come back to them over time. Choose one or two and commit to them. Then watch your life change before your eyes.

On Meditation is the second half to this part. In it, you'll find thoughts on meditation, my favorite practices, tips, and tricks. I make a point not to describe the actual experience of meditation because I don't think words can give it the proper respect. Trying to describe what meditation is like usually makes it more confusing. Instead, I set you up so that you can sit down, close your eyes, and experience it for yourself. It will be truer this way. Ten breaths are worth ten thousand words.

12 WAYS TO NOW

Don't Let Your Past Keep You from the Present

> "OUR CULTURE INCLUDES ALL KINDS OF ILLUSIONS, LIKE TIME
> IS REAL AND THERE IS SUCH THING AS THE PAST, WHICH IS
> PURE HOKUM."
>
> **—ALAN WATTS**

It might sound like a stretch to say that there is no such thing as the past. But it's really all in how you look at it. Sure, things happened in the world before today. More than we can imagine. How we think about what's happened is a completely different story.

We all have a habit of defining who we are today in relation to our experiences. Sometimes we hold on to memories of things we've done well because they make us feel good about ourselves. Other times, we hold on to bad memories because we feel they were the fire that shaped the steel of our character. Our memories are intimate. They are unique to each and every one of us. So we cherish them. We hold them close. In many ways, we believe that we are our memories and our memories are us. No matter how much we want to believe, for better or worse, that our stories make us who we are, it isn't always the case.

See, our long-term memories are actually rather inaccurate. What we experience at any given moment is only a narrow slice of what is there. As our attention darts around, our brain begins to release most of what we perceive in less than a second. In an attempt to be efficient, our subconscious mind filters out a lot of details. Not surprisingly, the details our mind removes are often related to our personal bias. But wait, there's more. Remember earlier when we were talking about the brain rewiring itself? It happens when we recall a memory, too. Every time we have a memory, we recall information that is stored in many different places in the brain. During the act of reconstructing a memory, our brain often inserts false details. Then, our brain rewires the new stuck-together version of our memory as the fresh copy.

So, every time we think back to our life, we are literally rewriting, or rather rewiring, our own story. If this is the case, why do we allow ourselves to get caught in our past? What we have experienced throughout our lives has made us who we are today. All of it: the good, the bad, the traumatic and the transcendent. But none of this is what we are.

WHEN YOU DRIVE FROM ONE PLACE *to* ANOTHER, YOU **DO NOT** BECOME THE ROAD ITSELF. YOU ARE *the* RESULT *of the* JOURNEY.

It's tempting to use our past to hold ourselves back. When we do, we're able to feel sorry for ourselves, validate harmful behavior, judge people, and make excuses for not trying. I know. I've been through my share of nastiness and have done all of the above. Using the story of our past to define who we are today is only a way to stay blind to the present.

We can liberate ourselves from the weight of what we carry by simply deciding to set down the story of our past. It doesn't all have to be done today. You can drop it bit by bit. As you do, you will find that the present begins to shine through and that you are not your past. You are now. You are capable of being anyone and anything. You will feel light. Adventurous. Ready to live the new story that lies before you.

Be Kind to Everyone

"NO ACT OF KINDNESS, NO MATTER HOW SMALL, IS EVER WASTED."

—AESOP

When I talk to other podcast hosts, I like to ask them a simple question: What have you learned from speaking to so many incredible people? I like asking this question because I always get a different answer and it's never what I would expect. Recently, I was thinking about the answers I've gotten to this question over the years. It dawned on me to turn the question on myself. What have I learned from the people I've talked to?

I mean, I've worked my way into an incredibly lucky spot. I have the great fortune to speak with some of the brightest minds out there. Respected leaders in the fields of mindfulness, neuro-science, and philosophy let me pick their brains for an hour every week. What better way to learn more about what I like? An inter-esting thing about these people is that for the most part, they are all public figures. People know them as the one they see in enter-tainment mode while giving a lecture or being interviewed on a podcast. But I see a different side of them. I get to "look behind the curtain" before we get started and see what they are like without their public mask on.

So, what have I learned from talking to hundreds of trailblaz-ing experts? Beneath their achievements, they are all people, too. Almost without fail, there is a subtle personality shift when the mi-crophones start recording. When you see any of these experts giving a lecture or being interviewed, they are deep in their flow. If you see enough media from the same person, you begin to get a sense that who you see on YouTube is who they are. But it isn't. They're real people with real ups and downs like everyone else.

Regardless of the public mask that someone puts on, you never know what they're going through on the inside. It doesn't matter if it's a person you admire, someone close to you, or a stranger you pass in public. Being human means that we all have our fair share of rough patches. This is why I believe it is wise to be kind to everyone, as much as you can, all the time.

YOU NEVER KNOW WHAT YOUR SMALL, QUIET ACT *of* KINDNESS MIGHT MEAN *to* SOMEONE.

There have been days when I was feeling low and the simple, kind smile of a stranger stoked a warmth inside of me that made a real difference. I have no doubt that you've experienced the same thing. So why shouldn't we all pass around kindness as much as we can? It's free, easy, and truly can change the course of another human being's life.

How will being kind to everyone help you stay present-minded? Kindness is contagious. Warmth spreads. And what we put out into the world is what we get back. This might sound like positive thinking, but I'll show you that it is quite realistic.

As we go about our lives, we tend to bump into the same people over and over again. We see the same faces at work, school, our local coffee place, and so on. The way we impact each of those people, especially over time, leaves an impression. If you're always funny at work, then people will smile when they see you and get excited to laugh.

Say that you meet a longtime friend for breakfast every week. You know each other well. There's no armor and no time spent getting comfortable. You're both cool and dive straight into open conversation. Of course, the opposite is also true. When someone has a habit of being cynical, irritated, or overly dramatic, you come to expect that kind of behavior from them. That kind of anticipation makes you close off and become guarded.

The patterns of our behavioral expression represent who we are to the rest of the world. Here's where the beautiful part comes in. When you are kind to everyone, as much as you can be, all the time, kindness is what people know from you. That means that everyone you encounter in your life will not only be happy to see you but also open, warm, and ready to embrace your kindness with their own.

Before long, your entire world shifts. Everyone you recognize looks at you with a warm face and radiant eyes. The open flow of how you exist in the world becomes magnetic. And that positive force of nature pulls you straight to what is in front of you. You are delighted and drawn to engage with your experience. Because it is beautiful. It is the essence of life. It is now.

Honor Your Individuality

"TO BE YOURSELF IN A WORLD THAT IS CONSTANTLY TRYING TO MAKE YOU SOMETHING ELSE IS THE GREATEST ACCOMPLISHMENT."

—RALPH WALDO EMERSON

There are more people alive at this moment than we can imagine. And more are showing up all the time. I was watching a movie from the early 2000s recently. During an emotional scene, the lead actor mentions that his wife is "one of the six billion" people on Earth. That number caught me off guard. Only six billion people were on the planet less than fifteen years ago? I had to know for sure. So I did a little research on world population growth. The film was right. Our world population has grown by a billion and a half people in about fifteen years. According to recent statistics, there are about one hundred and thirty million people born every year. That's a lot of socks and underwear.

In the modern world, the Internet and social media are connecting us with one another more every day. This level of connectivity is an incredible human achievement. Thousands of people can watch the same livestream from someone's phone. Kanye is able to tell thirty million people whatever pops into his head while he's sitting in his kitchen. But like most incredible achievements, it is not without its downside. Our human need to belong, be seen, and represent ourselves in a positive way is often exploited by technologies like these.

Everyone wants to look their best when they know they're going to be seen. That's why we dress sharp when we know we are going to have our picture taken. We work off that extra five pounds before the summer season and rock a new pair of shoes on a night out. There's nothing wrong with looking fresh on special occasions. In fact, everything is right with it. Looking good usually makes you feel good. When you feel good on a big day, it gives you that extra magic that takes you to the next level.

Now that we live in a culture where everyone posts the best pictures of themselves all the time, there is a pressure to always seem perfect. Or at the very least, portray ourselves that way online. Our digital representation of ourselves has become a self-image contest. People take photos from the best angles, in the best moments, with the best caption they can think of. This is all fine. Maybe it is even an art, like an Andy Warhol dream that collapsed on itself. But when the way we represent ourselves is so starved of reality, it leaves everyone hungry.

THE MODERN **WORLD** HAS LEFT EVERYONE **FEELING LIKE THEY** AREN'T ENOUGH.

People don't feel attractive, wealthy, or successful because the depiction of life online is only of the best moments available. When you're on this side of the phone screen, you can see all the moments of your real life. The good, boring, gross, and beautiful. Seeing only the best moments of other people's lives and the full picture of your own can make you feel bad. It's like you're the only one who has a life with moments that aren't Instagram worthy.

False inadequacy makes us feel like we need to change who we are. The modern world urges us to mimic the best parts of other people's lives in an attempt to live in a way that isn't possible. The social media industry has exploited our attention. In essence, they have made us all feel bad about who we are only to sell more advertising. While they continue to influence elections and make billions of dollars, we're left to search for self-worth. We are pulled out of the present moment by these forces, time after time. This leaves us trying to fit in and find a way to feel like we are enough.

The spell that digital culture has cast on all of us might seem bleak and unbreakable. But it isn't. Like all magic, if you know the trick, the illusion vanishes. The secret is that every person on this planet, all seven and a half billion of us, feel smaller than we really are. We all feel like we need to do something special to be enough for others. The real truth of the matter is that we are all enough, right now, as who we are today.

Here's where it gets funny. We try to be a certain way based on how we think other people think. But those people are trying to be a certain way based on how they think we think. So, everyone is a few layers removed from what we all actually are. And what we are is beautiful. One of a kind. Invaluable.

See, each of us holds a very potent and special treasure. That gold is the story of our lives. No matter who you are, you have lived a life that hasn't been lived by anyone else in all of history. You were born into your family and inherited their genetics and traditions. The culture of the places you've lived has rubbed off on you. You've shared one-of-a-kind conversations and moments with the people you have known in your life. There is a specific collection of books, music, and movies that only you have seen. Everything that has made you who you are is a gift. It has given you the singular jewel of your personal perspective.

You are the only place that the rest of us can get your version of the world from. We need you. You have something to offer, something to share, an experience we don't yet understand. So, please, trust in who you are. Know that you, with all your gifts and flaws, are an invaluable source of wisdom in this world. Don't hide who you are from the rest of us.

HONOR YOUR INDIVIDUALITY. YOU'VE EARNED IT BY WALKING IN YOUR FOOTSTEPS.

Spending less time worrying about finding a way to fit into a morphing image of perfection will liberate your attention. You no longer have to spend time distracted, in your head, worrying if you fit in or if you're good enough. You know you are good enough because you are here. Alive. The freedom from the modern game will leave your heart and mind open to soak in what lies before you. The infinite richness of now.

Try New Things That Challenge You

> "OFTEN, ALL THAT STANDS BETWEEN YOU AND WHAT YOU WANT IS A BETTER SET OF QUESTIONS."
>
> —TIM FERRISS

We do a lot of exploring while we're growing up. I'm sure you can think back to several different style phases that you went through. I know I can. When I think back to some of my early fashion choices, I wish I would have let them remain distant memories. Sure, reflecting on some of our past explorations might be a little embarrassing. That doesn't mean that they aren't an important part of our journey. We were figuring out who we are. And that process usually isn't pretty.

We spend much of the early part of our lives testing the world. From the moment we can move our little baby hands, we grab our toes, taste our fingers, and pull on Mom's hair. About the time things in hand's reach are figured out, we can start crawling around. Then it's time to test a deeper part of the world. We push the fragile object off the shelf, taste the cat, and tug at Mom's clothing. As we grow and become more mobile, we continue to test the world. One layer at a time. Our exploration kicks into high gear when we become teenagers. It's not only time to test the physics of life, but authority, style, and perhaps the limits of our consciousness.

Even though the first few decades of exploring life often serve us equal helpings of gifts and challenges, the journey is worth it in the end. Eventually, we figure out what we actually like, who we are, and how we fit into the world.

Getting a sense of yourself allows you to let go of a lot of silly and bad behavior. You can stop trying so hard and begin to embrace what makes you happy. Doing this carves out your path and firms up your individuality. While that's great, and it is truly great, after a while, we have a habit of getting a bit too firm in who we are. We keep doing what we know makes us happy and stop exploring. When we no longer feel the need to try new things, our patterns go from being firm to being hard.

Getting too comfortable with the idea of who you are tends to come with a notion of "having it all figured out." In some ways, it makes sense for us to feel that way. We have lived a full life, gone out into the world, explored, and found our island of the self. The start of that is good, but the island part is the problem. When you get too deep into the pattern of who you are, the outside world starts getting scary. Things that don't exist in your little slice of the world feel foreign and threatening. Insulating yourself with your own preferences will give you a false sense of safety. You become king of your tiny island. And anything that isn't familiar to you will threaten your very idea of who you are.

Shutting down in the face of new experiences makes us numb to the fullness that life has to offer. Closing off is a way to ignore parts of life.

Doing this is the opposite of living in the present moment. It is a way of living in a sanitized idea of the past. When we refuse to taste new flavors, listen to new music, or travel to new countries, we limit our experiences. By limiting our experiences we are limiting ourselves.

When you get used to experiencing the same things over and over, you reach a point where you don't have to pay attention. You've been there, done that, know what's what, and can go on autopilot. Doing this makes your senses fade and your instincts dim. There's no reason to perk up and awaken your animal nature. Slowly, your light starts to fade. When you are dim, there's no radiant light to make your world shimmer.

On the other hand, if you open yourself up to new things, your senses have to switch on. Why do they switch on? Because there's new information coming in. You've got to sort it out, understand it, and see how you feel about it. Experiencing something new forces your mind to open. It pushes you right to the present moment because your attention is needed. Once again, you are the baby tasting the cat, the teenager taking the car out on his own, or the traveler stepping off a plane and onto fresh foreign soil. The electricity from new experiences sends a buzz through your nervous system. You light up. And your world shimmers.

Figuring out who we are is great. Essential. It is what becomes our foundation. But if our patterns get too hardened, we can limit ourselves. Keep a solid base, but always mix up your life and try new things. Taste strange foods. Travel to faraway places. Talk to new people who seem different from you. It is how to not only live, but to be alive. Ask yourself new questions. You might surprise yourself and come back with an answer you didn't even know you were looking for.

Get Serious About Self-Care

"LET FOOD BE THY MEDICINE AND MEDICINE BE THY FOOD."

—HIPPOCRATES

The power of a good diet is often undervalued. People grab lunch on the go so they can get in a few extra minutes at the office. Or sometimes they hit the drive-thru on the way home because they don't feel like cooking. They may be saving a little time, but what they're sacrificing isn't worth it. They are trading minutes for mindset. It took me what feels like forever to figure out how important it is to eat mindfully. Actually, it took me getting a little older and gaining some weight. One day when I looked in the mirror, it was clear that I needed to figure out what was happening with my ever-expanding belly.

When I started reading about nutrition, I was stunned at how ignorant I was. Maybe it's because I grew up in Texas, the place where people eat BBQ for breakfast. Or perhaps I was so distracted by other things in life that my physical health wasn't on my radar. Whatever the case, once I started eating better, something unexpected happened. My mind gradually became more clear and some of my negative emotions began to fall away. Finally, I made the connection that what I put in my body had a direct connection to the way I felt. I started making wiser food choices and no longer ate until I was full. I ate only what I needed. I felt light, energetic, and quick.

I made a commitment to eating well and exercising regularly. I started taking the supplements and vitamins that I could feel working for me. Sleep also became a revelation. I'd lived a long time with the belief that I'd sleep when I was dead. All you've got to do is pound a gallon of coffee throughout the day, then drink enough alcohol to fall asleep, right? Wrong. Once I started respecting my need for sleep and getting eight hours a night, I clicked into an even higher gear. I was getting optimized.

My mind shaped up along with my body as I continued my dedication to self-care. It was fascinating to feel, in a real way, how my mind and body were connected. One day I had a bit of an aha moment: a thought that seemed so obvious but somehow I'd never quite made the connection before. Sure, most of us know that what you put in your body changes the way you feel. But I'd realized that what you put in your mind changes the way you see the world.

WHAT YOU CHOOSE *to* FEED YOUR MIND HAS *a* REAL EFFECT ON HOW YOU THINK.

We absorb everything that stimulates us. You only need a subtle amount of sensitivity to see that this is true. If you spend time listening to voices arguing about politics, you're going to think in argumentative ways. Watching violent films will make you more apt to have violent thoughts. Listening to only aggressive music is going to leave you feeling edgy with your nerves fried. If you spend your nights with bummer drama films, you can be sure that you'll feel down the rest of the evening.

The fact that the mind works a bit like a sponge can be a useful feature. We just need to feed it the things that give it the proper nutrition. Think of it like you would your diet. What will happen if you eat fast food and drink bourbon milk shakes every night? You're going to gain weight, feel sluggish, and have a less-than-enthusiastic worldview. On the other hand, what will happen if you eat fresh whole foods and drink green superfood smoothies? You're going to look healthy, feel springy, and be ready to take on the world. So, think of what would happen to your mindset if you fed your mind a nutritious diet.

You can get rid of a lot of your anxiety, discomfort, and distraction by paying attention to your mental diet. Think of it like cutting bad fats and sugar from your thoughts. Horror movies, superviolent themes, angry music, and shows with endless chatter are all good examples of media that are high in sugar. Movies that make you laugh, music that makes you feel good, inspiring books, and conversations that get you thinking are all like whole foods. They give your mind the nutrition it needs to feel good.

You'll find when you start laying off the mental sugar you feel less anger, anxiety, and confusion. It may sound simple, but it is a real method of personal change. You get out what you put in. If there is no excess of sugar in your stomach to digest, your body has no sugar to feed into your system. If there isn't an excess of sour themes in your mind, your brain has no extra negativity to feed into your thoughts.

Of course, it's good to splurge sometimes. If we ate and drank nothing but kale and filtered water all day, that would create new kinds of problems. And we'd be missing out on all the incredible yet unhealthy food out in the world. Like with our bodies, the goal is to maintain a consistent and overall nutritious diet. But, if you like ice cream, you can treat yourself to it every now and again. It makes you happy and that's a crucial part of self-care. So, if you like gory horror movies where you see people get slashed to bits, treat yourself to them now and again. Just don't make a diet out of them and leave yourself wondering why you have a hard time sleeping at night.

Create Good Habits

"PEOPLE DO NOT DECIDE THEIR FUTURES, THEY DECIDE THEIR
HABITS AND THEIR HABITS DECIDE THEIR FUTURES."
—F. M. ALEXANDER

As sophisticated as many people are, we often have a hard time keeping the long game in mind. We choose to sacrifice value for instant gratification every day. This is no fluke in us as individuals. According to many studies by psychologists and economists, it is part of our design. Their research shows that given a choice between a small reward today and a large reward in the future, most of us would take the small one today. We do this because our brain discounts rewards that we have to be patient to receive. The further in the future our reward is, the more our mind discounts it.

This behavior is called *time discounting*. Economist Richard Thaler published a paper that shows we start dismissing the value of rewards only days in the future. A standard example is that if you offered someone $20 now or $100 in a year, most would take the $20 now. People aren't aware they are doing this. Their logic persuades them to believe that they're making a wise choice. Not taking the $20 today would be going against their instincts.

Let's set aside hypothetical situations. If you look at the choices we make in our lives, you can see that we time discount constantly. Sometimes we have that next cocktail even though we know it's going to steal rest and mental clarity from us tomorrow. We find reasons to put off exercise knowing we'll regret it when we slide our jeans on in the morning. During holiday dinner, it's a ritual to eat so much that you almost feel sick. People smoke cigarettes, ignore illnesses, and spend money on vacation instead of paying their credit card bill.

We don't intentionally time discount. It just sort of happens because it feels like it makes sense in the moment. But if we aren't careful, we can end up time discounting ourselves out of a fortune of personal growth. Going from one flimsy impulsive pleasure to the next starts you at zero every morning. You can live a month, year, or decade like this and get nowhere. People do it all the time. That way of life is a cycle of suffering. Fortunately, it's an easy one to step out of.

At one point in my life, I time discounted like there was no tomorrow. Literally. I thought the point of living in the present moment was to pack in as much excess as you could. I knew that any of us could die at any moment. So I thought I might as well live to the extreme today. In those days, I went out seven nights a week, drank as much as I could, and blew most of my money doing it. Pastries and Mexican food were a good way to shake off the hangovers. A 24-ounce coffee or two always got the engine running again.

The weird thing was that this mindset made sense at the time. I believed that we never knew what tomorrow held so the wisest, freest, most human thing to do was blow it out every day. But doing that to yourself is not living in the present moment. It's running from the past and fearing the future.

After I slept on a cold bathroom floor enough times, it dawned on me that tomorrow would, in fact, keep coming. So, I decided it would be smart to make sure that tomorrow was not prepackaged with suffering. I starting thinking about the future and making smarter choices. After a little practice, I discovered something interesting. It was a formula for growth that delivered real results.

Consistent Action + Time = Lasting Change

Ah, there it is. The reverse formula for time discounting. When we wise up and think larger than the fleeting pleasure of instant gratification, we can transform ourselves. It's even easier than we think, too. All you've got to do is pick an important change you'd like to see in your life. Next, find a single small step you can take toward it. Then be patient, trust the process, and repeat the step every day. If you do this, big, tangible change will start to show up in your life.

My logic clicked with this concept by thinking about life in broad and realistic terms. I recognized that the calendar kept on turning, regardless of whether I paid attention or not. Three months from now, I'd look at the date, and it would be three months later. And there I'd be. In the same spot in my life. The same problems making me unhappy. The same changes I wanted to make going unchanged. I knew that I couldn't make miraculous changes overnight. Life doesn't work that way. Nor should we expect it to. But I knew that if I worked at something I wanted to change a little each day, in three months, I'd see real results. I was right. I started making big changes and it was so simple.

Let's say you get inspired and decide you'd like to hone your cooking skills. You're not going to be able to walk into the kitchen that night and whip up a perfect *croquembouche*. But, if you practice a little every evening, you're going to wake up in three months with real culinary skills.

This is the process of building intentional growth habits.

ANY CHANGE
THAT YOU
WANT *to* MAKE
IN YOUR LIFE
is POSSIBLE *and*
RIGHT AT YOUR
FINGERTIPS.

For real. All you have to do is look at the big picture, do something small toward it every day, and remember the formula:

Consistent Action + Time = Lasting Change

Intentional growth habits are a tremendous way to build mindfulness into your life. Think about it. You can start meditating for five minutes every morning. Choose to not look at your phone every other time you feel the urge. Make sure to not say judgmental things when they pop up in your mind. Any of these actions and more can become daily practices. Then, three months pass. Then another. And there you'll be. Looking at the calendar. But it won't only be you sitting there. It will be a lighter and brighter version of you. The kinder and more joyful you that you imagined all those months ago.

Do It Now

"THE SECRET OF GETTING AHEAD IS GETTING STARTED."
— MARK TWAIN

The War of Art: Winning the Inner Creative Battle is a book by Steven Pressfield that shows people how to overcome their creative barriers. What makes the book interesting is that it isn't as much about creative block as it is about blocked creativity. Pressfield focuses on one of the most ruthless killers of creative progress. It is the force that pushes people away from their desk when they want to write. The reason we come up with that makes us paint later instead of now. The excuse to start your business next month instead of this evening. This force is called Resistance. It's that feeling that shows up inside us when we want to do something, but for some reason just can't seem to get started.

I've felt this feeling plenty in my creative life. It's the worst. Especially when you're inspired. It feels like you and your workspace are both made of magnets. The problem is that all the magnets are the same side. When you go to dive into your work, there is a force pushing you away. You can't seem to lock in and get started. The struggle is tiring and you can only fight it for so long. You start psyching yourself out and come up with a reason not to start your creative work. Resistance wins and your creativity goes unexpressed.

Resistance doesn't only show up in our creative lives. It shows up everywhere. Anytime that we want to start doing something but don't, resistance is overtaking us. This self-defeat from not starting can keep us from getting even the simplest things done. We put off doing our laundry, wait until the last day to do our taxes, and never get around to learning a second language.

What's confusing about Resistance is that much of the time we actually want to do what we're putting off. You might be excited to wake up on a Sunday morning and paint. But when you find yourself standing by your paintbrushes you feel intimidated. Your mind is as blank as the canvas in front of you.

The base of our Resistance is fear. We are scared to open up, give ourselves over to the work, and put our ideas out there for others to see. The vulnerability of sharing what's in us is unnerving. Even if we're putting it out there for only ourselves to see. But this feeling of Resistance is a trick of the mind.

We're driven to create because we have something to say. Emotions and ideas have mixed together and grown inside of us. Inspiration is the feeling of our ideas pushing on our insides. They are asking us to let them out. Resistance is the dam we put up to hold in our expression. We feel fear when our inspiration gets so strong that it starts making the dam crack. We trick ourselves into thinking that it might be embarrassing if the dam breaks. But every time the dam gives, your ideas and emotions flow out into the world like a river. And it feels damn amazing. It's a relief. The pressure is gone. You're light. You also feel energized. That's because you're being fed. You have emptied yourself and are naturally being filled up with life again.

We meet Resistance all the time while trying to live mindfully. Even though we know that being present-minded will make us more peaceful, open, and compassionate, we still find reasons to put it off. We believe we're too busy to think about the present. We convince ourselves that we're too stressed to relax. Or maybe we fear that making our growth a priority will alienate a few friends. These are ways that we trick ourselves into nonaction. Just like creative Resistance, these excuses are holding you back from flowing into the world.

A friend recently asked me what my ritual is for meditating. I replied by saying, "My ritual for meditating is to sit down and meditate." There's nothing special you have to do before you start bringing more presence into your life. You've just got to take action. It's as simple as that. When Resistance dares you to find an excuse to walk away from your inspiration, you can beat it by walking into it. Resistance is an illusion. When you take a single step forward, you end up walking right through it.

Legendary jazz pianist Herbie Hancock gave profound advice on how to overcome Resistance. He said it in reference to music, but it snaps right into life: When you sit down at the piano, you shouldn't think about writing a song.

JUST PLAY *the* FIRST NOTE.

Don't think about it. Stick your hand out and press a piano key. Once you do that, you've already started doing it. You cut through Resistance and your creativity has begun to flow out into the world.

We make getting started way too complicated. Adding more presence to our lives gets overthought and made way harder than it needs to be. We will find reasons to put it off and intend to change our lives tomorrow. But that's Resistance talking. And if you think like that, you'll never experience everything this moment has to offer.

There's nothing to wait for. Nothing to buy. No perfect time to start. Introduce small bits of mindfulness into your life today. Pause before you eat your dinner. Then take slow bites. Taste each individual flavor and feel every texture on your tongue. Take ten deep breaths right now. Meditate for five minutes before you go to sleep tonight. Give the next person you talk to your complete attention. Actually listen to them. Put your phone in another room for the next hour. Exhale, relax the muscles of your body, and soak in the abundance of this moment on Earth.

You can find the present moment in every day. It's there like a piano key waiting for you to press it. So, go on. Put your hand out. Play the first note. Listen to your sound. Let the dam of Resistance crumble so the full expression of your life can flow out into the world.

Connect with Your Friends

Modern life, with its endless content streaming and meal-delivery options, has made it easier than ever to be isolated. Sinking deep into the comfort of your own home is enticing, too. Your living space is like your own little universe. Once you close and lock your front door, you're free and untethered from everyone else. You can do whatever you want, look how you want, and be whoever you want. That voice in the back of your head telling you to be switched on is happily switched off. You can let go. Relax. Do nothing. Not be bothered by reality.

As great as solo recharge time is, getting in too much of it can cause problems. It's like soaking in a hot tub. Soaking for an hour is heaven. Doing it for a week would be disastrous. Journalist Sebastian Junger wisely summed up this point in his book *Tribe*. He writes that "human beings need three basic things in order to be content: they need to feel competent at what they do; they need to feel authentic in their lives; and they need to feel connected to others."

Sebastian couldn't be more on point. Humans are social animals. There is an ancient part of our brain that needs us to connect with others. Doing so gives us an actual biological reward. Recent studies have shown that our brain releases dopamine, a motivating feel good chemical, when we are social. Bonding with others is an ancient behavior. It's also a cornerstone of our well-being.

When you don't spend time connecting with other people, you start getting a little dried out. Friends give you positive feedback, inspiring energy, and the most important bonding reward of all: laughter. Connecting with friends pulls you into the present moment. When you're full of energy, playing and crying from laughter with a good friend, you can't resist being in the moment. Why would you want your attention anywhere else?

As you age, it can get harder to make time to hang out. Everyone has busy lives. We also get into a habit of expecting our friends to reach out to us instead of reaching out to them. Of course, when everyone is doing that, no one hears from anyone. You can beat this problem by building social bonding into your life. It might sound funny to schedule hangouts as an adult. But I promise that it works, makes life easy, and has massive benefits.

I meet a friend for breakfast on the same day every week. I also meet with another friend, on the same night, at the same time, each week for a hang. There's not even any communication about whether it's going down that week or not. I pull up around 7:30 p.m. on our night and he walks outside. We've been meeting once a week for more than ten years. In all that time, we've only missed a handful of hangs.

But how could meeting up with the same person every week for so long not get boring? What in the world do we do? Not much. And that's by design. We eat dinner, talk about our current creative projects, and what's going on in our lives. But, more important than anything else, we laugh. We goof around, get silly, make ridiculous inside jokes, and usually cry from laughter. Our time dedicated to being nowhere and connecting for no reason pulls us both right into the present.

Enjoy the Journey

"HAPPINESS IS THE ABSENCE OF THE STRIVING FOR HAPPINESS."

—ZHUANGZI

Our culture has a happiness problem. From early on, we're taught that happiness is something we need to go out and get. This is largely due to the fact that we live in a consumer-driven society. We allow material objects to represent value, success, and wealth. How could we not? Most of what we see in movies, social media, and the news are celebrities reinforcing the idea that objects are what make us happy.

Thinking beyond the idea that stuff gives us worth can be tough. Even if you don't believe it to be true. We're so steeped in this way of thinking that it can be hard not to register someone with a nice car as someone who is "doing well." The truth is that many people with nice cars can't afford them. They take out a loan from a bank to pay for it. And the irony is that the loan to buy the thing to make them look valuable is what puts them in debt.

People want to believe that getting stuff or attention is what makes them happy. I mean, Jay-Z has made almost a billion dollars from repeatedly telling us about his next big purchase. We like the fantasy. But when we dream about relaxing on a yacht in the South of France, we aren't actually dreaming about wealth. We are fantasizing that one day we might find a way to end our feeling of desire.

The problem with believing that wealth will make you happy is that it won't. Sure, having enough money to not feel stressed about paying your bills is a valuable thing. It is a luxury that removes a horrible type of pressure. If you're lucky enough to have some extra cash to spend on fun, that's a great thing, too. Disposable income gives your life a little wiggle room. However, the benefits of extra income only go so far. **Nature**, a top scientific journal, recently published a study on how much money will make you happy. Almost two million people from more than 150 countries were surveyed. The study showed that money stops providing well-being when someone earns more than $60,000 to $75,000 per year.

One of the reasons we have such a hard time finding happiness in things, status, or achievements is because we aren't wired to. Evolutionarily speaking, humans are wandering and seeking animals. We are designed to keep moving, gathering, and exploring our entire lives. We're also designed to not stay satisfied by a single achievement. This is a large part of what kept our species alive before civilization.

Think back to when humans were hunter-gatherers. If we had evolved to feel happy forever following one good day of gathering, we would gather food only once. And then we would starve. To keep something like that from happening, we're wired to not feel too good about anything for too long. This tendency in people is called the hedonic treadmill. It doesn't matter what we achieve, how much money we make, or even how many lives we save. We get used to it. The new level becomes normal. Then, we start looking for the next level because we legitimately feel like we haven't gotten anywhere.

Understanding that we're wired this way will allow you to stop chasing the idea that more, of whatever, will make you feel complete. Happiness isn't something we find. Remember, happiness is never on the menu, no matter how much we hunt and gather. So, how about we learn from our evolutionary past? What has been making us feel good for hundreds of thousands of years? We aren't looking for a destination. There's no amount of money or achievement that will ease our desire. What we are looking for is right in front of us.

We can find happiness in the present moment. By engaging with each step of our journey, we can feel an ancient kind of fulfillment. When we give our attention to the process of living, to both pleasure and pain, we give our animal mind what it needs. By appreciating the journey of living, we are free to wander, hunt, seek, gather, and feel the reward of being alive. Every single day.

Hang Out with People Who Know More Than You

"I WANT TO BE WITH THOSE WHO KNOW SECRET THINGS OR ELSE ALONE."

—RAINER MARIA RILKE

When I was younger, I spent a lot of time with people who were much older than me. I got started with this early on due to having an older brother. He was hanging around with his friends who were older, cooler, and freer than my friends. Even though he's only four years older than me, sixteen feels like a lifetime away when you're twelve. Hanging with him and his friends involved me in life situations I wouldn't have had access to otherwise. Like trying a cigarette for the first time while zooming down a back road in a car with the windows down and sunroof open, blasting *Kill 'Em All* by Metallica.

I got more from hanging around with my brother and his friends than new experiences. I was able to talk to people in high school.

They knew all sorts of things about life that I had no idea about. I could hear their slang, the stories of the trouble they'd got into, and what their plans were after graduation. Having a heads-up on high school stuff like this got me thinking about bigger things earlier. It made me confront my own life in a different way and with less fear. That was when I began to realize that it was wise to surround myself with people more knowledgeable than me.

Through a simple chat with someone who knows more than you, you're able to learn a ton. What's funny is that in a lot of ways, I've made a profession out of it. What do I do on my podcast? Talk to people who are leaders in the fields of study that interest me. I've learned so much from the guests who have come on my show, I could write a book about it. And in a way, parts of this book are exactly that.

As we move forward in our lives, we spend a majority of the time carving out our own way of seeing things. This is good. Developing an independent point of view is the only way to start understanding yourself. But the more we strengthen our own point of view, the harder it can get to look beyond your own way of seeing things. This is dangerous territory because there is a chance you'll stop listening to others. The clearest sign that you've stopped learning is when you feel like you have it all figured out.

Spending time with friends, family, and people who work in your field and are more knowledgeable than you is a surefire way to keep learning. The thing is, whoever you speak with doesn't have to have a wide scope of knowledge. Someone who knows a lot about a specific thing will have more to teach you than someone who knows a little about a lot of things. What's cool is that a conversation where one person is sharing specific knowledge with another is good for both people involved. You get to pick up a few new thoughts from someone with more experience. The person sharing with you is able to clarify their thoughts by expressing them in simple terms. And they're sure to learn a thing or two from you as well.

By finding these mini-mentors, you're able to pull yourself forward into new worlds of knowledge. This helps ensure that your point of view is always growing. And, of course, when you're searching to understand more about life, there is only one place you can be: right here and right now.

Don't Get Trapped in Your Thoughts

"TO KNOW YOURSELF AS THE BEING UNDERNEATH THE THINKER, THE STILLNESS UNDERNEATH THE MENTAL NOISE, THE LOVE AND JOY UNDERNEATH THE PAIN, IS FREEDOM, SALVATION, ENLIGHTENMENT."

—ECKHART TOLLE

One of our main causes of distraction is also one of our greatest strengths. We have the incredible ability to think about what we're thinking. As far as we know, humans are the only animal that can do this. Other animals operate from instinct. Before they know what they're going to do next, they're already doing it.

Of course, some more developed critters seem to be reflective. Some of them even seem self-aware. I know my wife and I often wonder if our dog knows more than he's letting on. But even a gorilla, an animal that is able to communicate with humans through sign language, falls short of our mental processing power.

It's pretty far out if you stop and think about it. We seem to be the only living animals on our planet that can think about our thinking. By gifting us with a large brain, Mother Nature set us apart from all other species on Earth. Our ability to think about our thoughts is what made a society that bends toward peace possible. Unlike our animal friends, we are able to understand the consequences of our actions in a deep way. This skill lets us choose love over hate and kindness over brutality. Without our level of self-awareness, we would be beasts, battling it out in the wild.

But with great powers comes great burden. Being able to think about what you're thinking means that you can endlessly reflect on negative thoughts. All of us do this at one time or another. When we feel down, we let bad thoughts about ourselves build up. If we're feeling anxious, we worry about our worries. When we're sad, we convince ourselves the feeling will never go away.

Getting trapped in your thoughts is like sitting in a waiting room of suffering. And because it puts you deep into your head, it reduces your awareness of the physical world around you. Of course, we will all have our moments where our thoughts get away from us. It is worth remembering that you are not your bad feelings. They are only passing through you. Think of bad states of mind like seasons. In the heart of winter, it's tough to believe you'll ever stop feeling cold. But the warmth of spring always comes around again. Sometimes it only takes minutes and other times it takes months. Trust that the warmth will come. The whole cycle is a part of our nature.

When you feel trapped in your thoughts of anxiety, pain, stress, or sadness, remember that they are not you. Those feelings are like snow covering grass. Watch them. Don't let yourself identify with the feelings and get wrapped up in them. Try making friends with them instead: "Hello, Sadness. There you are again. It is not nice to see you, but here you are. I will recognize you. See that you're there. Feel you for a moment. I won't get trapped below you, though. I'll appreciate you and let you have your season. I can do this, without dread, because I know that spring is coming fast."

Just Listen

"WHEN YOU'RE WIDE OPEN, THE WORLD IS A GOOD PLACE."
—SHARON SALZBERG

People are fascinating. They really are. There are a lot of us on this planet. Because of that, we can sometimes see people as clutter. Another person in front of you in line or taking your parking spot might feel like a roadblock. They aren't. They are a doorway to another universe.

I want you to do something the next time you talk to someone: Ask a simple question about the person. Then listen. I mean, really listen. Don't just listen to what they are saying, but listen to where they are saying it from.

You are an original. So is everyone else. That's the beauty of being alive. Every time you talk to someone, they can tell you something about our world that you have no way of knowing. People are like living paintings. Each time they share their point of view they are painting a picture of how they see reality. This is why it's so important to stay open. Don't assume you know what others think. Try to fill in as few blank spaces as possible. Be open. Listen and let your mind bend when someone speaks to you. Then sit back and soak in their humanity.

Imagine what you know about the world as your personal museum of ideas. Every time you listen deeply during a conversation, you're gathering new perspectives on life. These ideas and points of view are like works of art that you can add to your collection. The more effort you put into hearing what people tell you, the more comprehensive your museum of ideas will be.

Staying open to what others share will keep you in touch with the present. It will expand how you are able to think about your life. When you are patient and allow yourself to understand where other people are coming from, you can learn about new ways to see the world. Doing this doesn't only make your present moment expand. It makes your way of seeing life become new time and time again.

ON MEDITATION

Being There

Meditation is one of the best ways to reduce anxiety, relieve stress, and focus your mind. It's natural and people have been doing it for thousands of years. How has it been able to stand the test of time? Why has it recently surged in popularity? Because it works. You can drop into meditation anytime, anywhere, and create a real change in the way you feel. Meditation is a powerful, life-changing practice. And all it costs you is a few minutes a day.

We have a tendency to make simple things more complicated than they are. It's hard for us to accept when ideas are simple because most things in life seem so complicated. This can make trusting a simple idea feel counterintuitive. How could something as basic as focused breathing improve our health? There has to be more to it, right?

People overcomplicate things because it allows them to leave their fingerprints behind. Meditation is easy to make more difficult than it is because it is a practice based in the mind. It's a process of ideas that develops through experience. This makes how we think about meditation slippery because there is no empirical guide to use as a reference. When you start eating a healthier diet, you can see your body change and measure it by how your clothes are fitting. But the majority of change from meditation is in how you think and feel. We can't hold and weigh our results. We have to check in with how we are feeling and the way our outlook has changed. That's why it is easy to complicate.

Through history, people have written millions of words trying to describe the experience of meditation. Only a handful of those people have been able to touch the feeling in a way that transfers it through the pages. Those words are powerful and transformative, and have become classic. Then there's the rest of what has been written about meditation. Those texts are often abstract, imprecise, and add to the general confusion on the topic. Of course, these books may have useful tidbits. But they tend to add a lot of extra miles to the journey.

I want to share an example with you in case you've read about meditation before and felt confused. This will show you why it's hard to describe an intimate first-person experience to someone else. It will also point to why it wasn't your fault if you got lost. Imagine trying to write about what you would experience, from your point of view, if you were to stand up, walk into your kitchen, and pour a cup of coffee. It would be easy to write out a description of that event from the outside as if a camera had filmed it. But what would it take to describe your experience, with such accuracy that another person could read it and actually feel what you felt? You'd need to somehow convey the history of memories in your house, your life experience, and how you view the world. Doing that would be hard. Really hard. Even the greatest writers of our time confront this problem.

That is the problem with writing about meditation. People try to describe the actual experience, and it is no easy task. You've got to be half poet and half engineer to even have a chance. And that's a rare combination. This is too bad because this is the kind of thing that keeps people from developing a meditation practice. So many people decide to give meditation a shot, then quickly feel lost, intimidated, or like they're doing it wrong. I want to end that confusion here.

I'm going to do my best to clear the haze around meditation and talk about it in as few words as possible. I'll talk about experiences around meditation, but I am not going to try to describe the experience itself. What I will do is offer some thoughts and techniques on meditation so that you can try it. That way, you can cut to the chase and simply get to the experience. But before we dive in, I'd like to share a little backstory with you so that you'll know where I'm coming from.

I've been studying and practicing meditation for about twenty years. It has added immeasurable value to my life and continues to do so every day. As we touched on earlier in the book, my mind was full of hot thoughts when I was young. I was bursting with anxiety, emotional pain, and spiraling concepts. It was awful. My stomach turned and my hands sometimes shook when I went to put the key in my front door because I was so anxious. I searched for anything that would relieve the tearing I felt in my chest. I knew there had to be some way I could soothe my inner life and I decided to look until I found it.

I've always enjoyed teaching myself as much as I can about things that interest me. I love learning because I believe that as you grow, your world grows. While I was in a deep stride of teaching myself about Eastern philosophy, I came across a lot of writing on meditation. What it offered sounded good. Magical actually. So I started trying basic techniques alone in the privacy of my bedroom. This felt safe. When I was alone, with the door closed, I could put down my guard and let my inner and outer lives touch.

My early meditation efforts couldn't have been more simple. I would lie down on my bed, close my eyes, take slow, deep breaths, and try to relax my body as I exhaled. I remember instantly feeling more calm and clearheaded. Honestly, if you only did this for ten minutes each morning, you would notice real positive shifts in your mindset.

I don't believe that there is a correct way to meditate. There are different ways of doing it and the only thing that makes it right is if it works for you.

MEDITATION IS YOUR PRACTICE.

It is as personal as a piece of clothing. It should fit you well and make you feel good. You should want to do it again. It isn't a chore. It is a gift.

A meditation style isn't anything mysterious. It's a collection of techniques for sitting, breathing, and reflecting. Over the years, I tried every method I could find. As I experimented with different approaches, I paid attention to the way they made me feel. When a certain way of sitting or breathing felt good to me, I would include it as an option to use in my practice. This is how I created my own style. My suggestion is for you to do the same.

One of the intriguing qualities of meditation to me is that it has an endless amount of potential. You can feel results the first time you try it. A calmness, clarity, and openness begin to awaken in your life. From there, it continues to get more expansive. What's important to remember is that it isn't a contest. You don't have to go deeper than the next person. There is no "more" in meditation. There is only where you are in that moment. If you're drawn to getting deeper into your meditation practice, that's great. If all you need is a touch, then that's fine, too. Because you only need to go where you need to go. Not where you think other people think you need to go.

Personally, I like searching for the bottom of the ocean every now and then. I'm still pleasantly surprised by what I discover in my meditation all the time. Just when I think I've found the deepest layer of personal insight, I pass through to a new one. This has happened over and over for decades and I don't expect it to stop in this lifetime. If there's one thing I've learned, it's that there is no bottom to meditation.

MEDITATION *is* AS DEEP AS **YOUR** **MIND** BECAUSE IT *is* YOUR MIND.

About fifteen years into my practice, something broke loose inside of me. It had taken a while, but I had finally given myself over to my meditation. I had stopped grasping. It was liberating. For weeks I would sit on my cushion meditating with tears quietly rolling down my cheeks. They were the tears of sadness I had held back my entire life. When the sadness had drained, those tears were replaced with soft tears of joy. I was overwhelmed with a gratitude for my own existence and felt a warmth blossoming within me. My heart was taking off its armor.

After that, I would meditate without trying to achieve anything. I let go and allowed myself to simply be there, right where I was, right then. One day, as I sat on my cushion, the slightest smile crept up my face. You probably couldn't have seen it if you were looking at me. But I could feel the corners of my mouth moving upward in the subtlest of ways. Peace was resting on my face. I wasn't trying to wear a smile. A smile had come from somewhere else to wear me.

When I felt that liberation, the freedom of my own peaceful presence, I wanted it for other people. My meditation practice had always been something private and personal. But at that moment, it dawned on me that I needed to share my journey. My path had been a gift of such personal transformation and I hoped that others could receive the gift, too. I began teaching a series of guided workshops in my hometown of Austin. Eventually, I made the material accessible worldwide by creating an online meditation course.

I've had hundreds of personal interactions with students. They're always excited to share which methods have worked best for them. Hearing so much feedback gave me an insight into which of the practices I offered were the most effective. These methods and perspectives are what I'm going to share with you next. First, we will explore ways of thinking. Then we will dive into ways of doing.

My sincere hope is that you can use these techniques to ease your suffering and bring more peace into your life. And I believe that you will.

MEDITATION is NOT HARD. YOU DO IT EVERY NIGHT WHILE YOU SLEEP.

I am just going to show you how to do it while you are awake.

Meditation Is a State of Mind

When I talk about meditation with someone who isn't familiar with it, they often feel three things: Curiosity. Intimidation. Yearning. In a sense, sharing stories about your meditation practice is like telling someone about a dreamy foreign vacation. In both cases, you see new things, learn about yourself, and mix up your life patterns. You also let your mind charge up with wonder.

If you'd like to try meditating but feel intimidated or unsure, I promise you haven't got anything to worry about. You'll do great. I've never heard of anyone who has regretted going on a trip of a lifetime. And likewise, I've yet to hear of anyone who has wished they had not started meditating.

THE ESSENCE *of* MEDITATION *is* SITTING *and* BREATHING.

All you have to do is sit down, close your eyes, rest your hands on your legs, and focus on your breath moving in and out. If you only did this for fifteen minutes a day, you would notice a big change in the way you feel.

We contract as we take on the stress of the day and carry the weight of our responsibilities. This pressure builds up over time, without us noticing it. And then one day, something happens, and we realize that we've become an uptight ball of nerves, contracted, tense, and hypersensitive. Practicing meditation helps you expand. It's a short moment in your day where you can calm your mind, relax your body, and come back to center. Then an interesting thing happens once your sitting practice becomes consistent. You start seeing life from a different point of view.

Your meditation cultivates an abundance of breathing room—an open space where you can feel expansive, clear, and grounded.

One of the great benefits of meditation is being able to calm your frustration and anger. The self-awareness of meditation allows you to recognize damaging feelings before they take you over. You can let them pass through. Flow in and flow out. I'm not saying you won't feel those things anymore. You will, but the time it takes to feel normal again will be cut down. Maybe in half. Or even into seconds. Think of how precious that time could be. Imagine what spending less time in an angry state might save you from thinking, saying, or doing.

Meditation is a short daily practice, but its lasting value is that it becomes your default state of mind.

EVERY TIME YOU PRACTICE, YOU EXPAND YOURSELF.

Over time, this expansion exceeds your daily contraction. When this happens, you have more breath than the stress of the daily grind can push out of you. The ease of pressure gives you the ability to respond to your life instead of react to it. It helps you slow down the movie of your life so that you can see every frame.

When you try meditating for the first time, you might find that you feel a little fidgety. But I assure you that it will get easier to sit restfully after a few go-rounds. Most people are always doing something with their hands to keep busy. Maybe they are poking at their phone, twirling their hair, clicking a pen, fiddling with a ring, bouncing a leg, or something similar. These physical fidgets represent a person's mental chatter. Think of a philosopher leaning back, stroking their beard long and slow. Somehow you can tell they are in deep thought. They are calm, collected, and focused in their physical expression. Their movements show us the state of their mind.

In our modern world, we simply aren't used to not moving for more than a few seconds. The first time you sit and try to meditate, it will feel weird to rest your hands on your legs. You'll want to move them. It will feel like you need to. Your mind will make up a reason for you to move. Almost like you are addicted to fidgeting. But don't. Acknowledge the suggestion from your mind to move and then let the thought go. Take an exhale. Relax your muscles.

After a handful of practices, the desire to move your hands passes. You'll find that you are comfortable sitting there, relaxing in your body. It's entertaining to watch your fidgeting melt away. You'll be able to see how your busy hands were acting out your mental chatter.

WHEN YOU GET
COMFORTABLE
RESTING YOUR
BODY, YOUR
MENTAL
CHATTER
WILL REST, TOO.

Yet it might not seem like your mental chatter has quieted. If anything, it could feel like it's gotten worse. This is a misunderstanding. One that often makes people feel like they are doing something wrong. You aren't. This may sound odd, but what has happened is that your mental chatter has quieted enough for you to get a real look at it. It's like driving through a thick fog. Only when the fog lets up enough for you to see the horizon do you get a sense of how much fog you're dealing with.

Remember when we compared an international vacation with meditation? Well, let's take a look at how the lasting benefits they share are connected.

YOU SEE NEW THINGS.

When you calm your mental chatter you gain a sense of the world outside of yourself. Being less self-focused allows you to see things from a larger perspective. Meditation makes the spotlight of your awareness expand from only you to all around you. It's like standing under a streetlight and having the sun come up. A new world of potential arises from the darkness of distraction.

YOU LEARN ABOUT YOURSELF.

Thinking of your life in larger terms allows you to be self-reflective with greater ease. By reflecting more, you are able to understand how you engage with your life and treat other people. Self-awareness of this kind allows you to refine your behavior and bring your best self forward.

YOU BREAK OUT OF LIFE PATTERNS.

Seeing the big picture more clearly helps you understand the patterns in your life. Bad habits, toxic relationships, and restricting paths become clear. Once you identify parts of your life that aren't serving you well, you are able to step out of harmful patterns of behavior.

YOU RESTORE YOUR MIND.

Seeing the world in new ways tends to make you realize that you don't and can't know everything. This is quite a wonderful revelation to have. People think this all the time. But to feel it is something else. When you do, it makes life exciting. When you know that you don't know it all, you know there's always more to learn. Your hunger to learn, drink in life, and continue expanding your mind becomes unquenchable.

THE BEST PART ABOUT KNOWING **YOU DON'T KNOW** EVERYTHING *is* THAT YOU DON'T **FEEL LIKE YOU** KNOW MORE THAN OTHER **PEOPLE.**

An attitude like that is what makes the mind fertile for the growth of wisdom.

Meditation doesn't make all these things happen overnight. But the more you practice, the more they will show up. Eventually, this sense of spacious self-awareness will grow into a natural part of who you are.

Growing mindful awareness is like learning to play an instrument. When you first pick up a guitar, you can make plinking sounds but can't play a song. After some practice, you get a few chords down and can string them together into a tune. Before you know it, you can grab your guitar and start playing a song without thinking about it. You feel it and it comes out of you.

When you're learning how to play guitar, you aren't figuring out chords one day, a switch flips, and then all of a sudden you're Jimi Hendrix. It's a gradual process. The growth sneaks up on you. The benefits of meditation come on in the same way. What's different is that the growth takes place in your mind. Because of this, the way you see the world begins to change, and that changes everything around you.

Breathe Like You Are Sleeping

BREATHING

BREATH *is the* TEMPO *of* OUR BEING.

We know that it is important to breathe well, but we often don't think about why. The depth of our breath has an incredible impact on our mindset. Somehow, we already know this. Even if we haven't put words to the connection between breath and mind, we can feel how they work together. Like our heartbeat, our breath flows from the oldest part of our brain. These things are involuntary. Upstream of logic or will.

How we breathe reflects our personal experience like a mirror. A person resting in the depths of sleep will take slow and patient breaths. Someone suffering from a panic attack will take short and panicked breaths. They'll look as if they are drowning without a drop of water in sight.

OUR BREATH CAN BE OUR TEACHER.

By paying attention to it, we can be more in tune with the way we feel. This is especially useful during challenging moments. When you are in a stressful situation, there is a good chance that your pulse and breathing will be elevated. If you've made it a habit to check in with your breath every so often, you'll notice that you've slipped into an anxious state. After recognizing the rushing of your body, you can start taking slow and deep breaths. Doing this will help your mind relax and bring your body back into balance. We know if our breath is slow and deep that we will be calm. But sometimes, we get distracted and caught up in the momentum of anticipation. In times like these, we need to reset ourselves.

Of course, stressful situations aren't the only places we should be mindful of breathing deep. We should also practice taking long and slow breaths during our meditation. Doing this will help us get to a state of mind that is more restful than we are used to. When we spend time in relaxed mental states, they tend to rub off on us. That's how we can carry them forward into our life.

Keeping your back straight while meditating will help you breathe by moving your chest forward and relaxing your shoulders. A posture such as this reduces your resistance to breathing in by opening up the muscles in your chest.

Even though you should be mindful to take long and slow breaths while meditating, it should not feel unnatural. You don't want to exaggerate or force your breath. Simply allow it to deepen in an intuitive way. Think back to the image of how a healthy person breathes while they are sleeping. It is calm and deep, but still totally natural. Someone who is asleep can breathe with such depth and ease because they aren't resisting. They are allowing the breath process to flow without their mind getting in the way.

Try this technique if you have trouble getting into a deep state of breathing:

- Slowly expand the bottom of your stomach as you start breathing in.

- When your stomach goes out as far as it can, continue inhaling and roll the expansion upward until the top of your chest extends to its limit.

- Hold your breath there at full capacity for one beat—half a second.

- Calmly start pulling your stomach in as you exhale and gently roll upward again until all the air is pushed out.

- Repeat this cycle until you find the space needed to take naturally deep breaths.

Here's an interesting fact about breathing. You don't have to try to exhale. The body is designed to exhaust the oxygen that it's holding automatically. So, after you take a deep breath, you can simply let your chest fall. Your body will push your breath on its own.

Fun fact: The atmosphere of our planet is pressurized. When you take a breath in, you are "taking" a breath out of the atmosphere and into your body. All you've got to do to return it is let go!

Your breathing habits will begin to shift as you practice meditation more consistently. The expansive way of breathing that you practice during meditation will start to show up in your daily life. One day, you'll find that you've begun to breathe deep and slow almost all the time. The body wants breath and will happily change its standard of depth if you provide the extra air.

SITTING

There are a variety of tried-and-true ways to sit while you're meditating. What's important is that you find one that feels comfortable to you.

You don't need to rush out and buy a *zafu* and *zabuton* (pillow and cushion used for meditation). If you find that meditation is something that you enjoy, I would recommend getting a set eventually. Meditation pillows make the experience much more delightful. They also work as a constant visual reminder to plop yourself down and soak up some peace. For now, you can grab a pillow and find a comfortable spot on the floor.

People often think of Full Lotus pose when they imagine someone meditating. This is when you sit cross-legged but with one heel pulled up on the opposing thigh and the other heel pulled up on the other opposing thigh. The hands then rest on the knees, palms up. The pillow goes under your butt to help keep your spine straight. Full Lotus takes some practice to get into and isn't good for people who have nagging knee issues. Full Lotus is the posture that has become the caricature of meditation in the cultural mind. But it is certainly not mandatory.

Pro tip: Don't force uncomfortable postures. In the big picture, what's the point? If a posture is so uncomfortable that it keeps you from meditating, then it is removing potential benefits, not adding them.

A less intense version of Full Lotus is called Half Lotus. This is when you sit cross-legged but with only one heel pulled up on the opposing thigh. The pillow still goes under your butt to keep your spine straight and your hands rest on your knees, palms up. Ah, now we're talking. This posture is much more forgiving on the body for beginners or people with any knee or leg problems. This is how I have begun sitting more often over the past year. I like to mix up how I sit when my body calls for change. Doing this helps keep things fresh. After you try a few ways of sitting, you will discover that they each offer something different and that cycling through them can be useful.

You can also sit cross-legged. Hands resting on your knees, palms up. Simple and effective. One issue that arises with this is that it can cause your lower back to soften and this can make your back hunch. So make sure to have a pillow under your butt to give your spine a little help with staying straight.

Now, another favorite position of mine: *Seiza*. It sounds exotic. It's not. It is a Japanese term for a traditional way of sitting in Japan. *Seiza* is a kneeling position. Imagine being on the floor, on your knees. Start there. You then put a pillow behind you, between both of your feet. Sit back onto the pillow and open your knees into a slight *V* shape until it's comfortable. Your hands then rest on your thighs. In this position, I keep my hands palms down. This position works well for me when my back is hurting. The way that the legs and hips create a foundation in *Seiza* seems to support the spine especially well.

Don't despair if sitting on the floor isn't up your alley. You can meditate while sitting in a chair or even lying down. This is a helpful approach for people who have injuries, too. We all have different-shaped bodies. The same thing is not going to work for everyone. Experiment until you find what feels natural. The correct way is what feels best for you and makes you want to do it again.

BUT WHEN?

Carving out the time to meditate is one of the most important parts of the practice. I've had an enormous number of people reach out and ask me what time of day they should meditate.

The best way to get consistent with your practice is to build it into part of your routine. That way, it doesn't become something you always feel like you're juggling and trying to find time for. That can make it feel like a chore. Also, when you meditate a few days in a row, you start to feel motivated by the compounding benefits.

I like meditating in the morning after a cup of coffee. This ensures that I've had some time to wake up and get my mind going. I also like to quickly glance at my schedule so that I don't worry that I am forgetting something important. You know, meetings with the Dalai Lama, chats with Elon Musk about going into space, emails from the Pulitzer Prize committee, things like that.

Another reason I like meditating in the morning is that it helps set the tone for my day. Afterward, I am noticeably more focused, calm, clearheaded, and comfortable in my own skin. It's important to me to take on the day with my optimal self. If you want to do your best, you have to feel your best.

There are many people who like meditating before bed because it helps them relax and get to sleep. I don't have problems falling asleep. I'm one of those lucky "turn off the light switch of my mind" type of people. But, I do sometimes do a short relaxation practice while lying in bed with the lights off. It's one of my favorite mini-practices and I'll share it later on.

Try just picking a time. First thought, best thought. We waste so much time in our lives trying to make simple decisions. We usually end up spending more time thinking about doing something than it would take to actually do it. Like scrolling through Netflix looking for a show to watch until you don't want to watch anything anymore. So just add meditation to a place in your routine. If that doesn't feel like it's working, move it to another spot in the day until it feels right. Eventually, you'll find your groove.

One to Ten and Over Again

To get our feet wet, I'm going to share a meditation technique that's straightforward and effective. It's unique in that it works equally as well for long meditation sessions as it does for short ones.

I've been ending my meditations using this technique for years. It's come to be a good meter to gauge how calm and focused my mind is.

Start by finding a comfortable position to sit in. Perhaps one of the positions that I described in the earlier section will come in handy. Of course, you're more than welcome to use a sitting posture of your own. What is important in a posture is that it feels natural and you are well supported.

Your legs and butt should feel like a foundation. Take note of the spacing of your knees, where your heels are, and how your hips are rotated. Experiment with your posture until it feels solid and effortless.

You will want to make sure that your chest is slightly forward and open and that your shoulders are relaxed. Your spine should flow upward like it's growing out of your hips. The spine should be straight, but not unnaturally so. Then, allow your head to lightly float on top of your body like a balloon.

Let out a deep exhale once you are seated and comfortable in a well-balanced position.

Close your eyes.

Direct your attention toward your breath. Become aware and focus on the soft rising and falling of your chest. Begin taking slow, deep breaths. You don't want to force it; let it feel natural but allow it to become deeper and slower. Breathe like you are sleeping.

As you begin to get comfortable and allow yourself to relax
in your body, start to release the tension in your muscles. You
might be surprised at what you find.

Tension held in muscles reflects tension held in the mind. Most
of us carry a good deal of tension in our bodies without realizing it.
Daily stress causes us to clench, creating a muscular armor with
which to bear the blows of life. We tend to forget to take the armor
off. Eventually, the muscle clenching becomes an instinctive bad
habit.

Begin scanning your body. Identify places where you find
clenched muscles. As you exhale, relax those muscles. Then,
continue searching your body for more tension.

Continue locating tension in your body and releasing it with
an exhale. Do this until you feel like you are free from resting
tension.

Make sure that you relax the muscles in your face. The brow,
cheeks, jaw, and throat are notorious tension reservoirs. Another location for serious clenching is the shoulders. Most of us tighten and
raise our shoulders when we get stressed. Doing this contracts the
upper body and makes it hard to breathe. Shallow breath makes us
more stressed. Shoulder clenching can keep us locked in a momentum of anxiety.

Once you release these major tensions, you might notice lighter
tension in your arms, hands, legs, and stomach. Move your attention

to these more subtle areas. As you notice tension, release it with an exhalation. After calming your muscles, a feeling of lightness will wash over you.

Relax into your body with a good exhale. With your eyes closed, point your attention back to your breath.

I want you to solely focus on the feeling of your chest rising and falling with each breath. Sit there for a few breaths and just pay attention to your chest moving up and down.

Remember: While you are meditating, this is your personal moment in time. Any stress, worry, deadline, or obligation can be dealt with later. This is what you are doing now. The only thing. And it is for you.

With your eyes closed and your body relaxed, point your attention to your breath. Observe it moving in and out, your chest calmly moving up and down.

This is the fun part.

Start counting your breaths in your head. Don't rush.

An inhale and an exhale, one.

An inhale and an exhale, two.

An inhale and an exhale, three . . .

See if you can count to ten without losing count. If your mind wanders and you realize you have stopped counting, start over at one again. If you get to ten, start over at one again.

Continue sitting, with your eyes closed, counting your breaths until you can reach ten.

Your mind will sharpen the more you practice this simple technique. It's like a gym for your attention. Don't feel bad if you have trouble counting to ten breaths without getting distracted. I have guided hundreds of students through this practice and only a handful of them were able to count to ten on the first try. After a few tries, you'll get to ten without even trying.

I like to use this breath-counting technique at the end of my meditation session. It's a good way to make sure my mind is as calm and focused as I'd like it to be. If my mind wanders somewhere in the counting, I know that I need to sit a while longer.

This practice works well when you are grabbing a quick mini-meditation during the day. You can use it any time you find yourself feeling contracted. Sitting at your desk, on an airplane, or standing in line are all good opportunities. All you need to do is pause, close your eyes, relax your muscles, and deepen your breathing. Then, count ten inhales and exhales a single time. It's a powerful refresher that I end up using almost every day.

Until the Peace Comes

How long should I meditate? This is a question that raises a good deal of uncertainty for most meditators. I think the reason why it's so challenging for people to find an answer is because there is not one. There is no "correct" amount of time to meditate.

You'll find no shortage of people who say the ideal length to meditate is twenty, thirty, or sixty minutes. There are people who also say that two hours is ideal. My opinion, based on my experience, is that thirty minutes is a good target length. Of course, you should listen to your intuition and do what's best for you. Meditation is about getting your mind and body connected with the present. Not the clock.

Ideally, we should all be able to meditate without worrying about time. Realistically, life is built on circumstances. Most days, you've got somewhere to be. So, you won't always be able to meditate without time in mind. If you are short on time, you might find it useful to set a timer before meditating. It can help you relax if you know you can count on the alarm to keep you from being late. There's nothing wrong with making meditation work for you. In fact, it should.

People ask me what kind of meditation alarm I use. It's nothing fancy. It's as basic as it gets. I use the timer on my iPhone. It's handy because once the iPhone timer is done, it resets to the original amount of time you set to countdown. That prevents you from having to dial up your desired amount of time each day.

Meditation is fluid. That's one of its most curious strengths. It can be long, short, deep, shallow, emotional, or intellectual—all at once, one at a time, or anywhere in between.

Here are my suggestions for some meditation lengths to aim for if you're meditating in a time crunch. I've also included my thoughts on what the amount of time will provide you:

- 5 minutes: A quick meditation like this definitely shakes the rust off. It's worth every second and will provide a 10 percent improvement in your day. If this is all you can find time for in your morning, it is still of tremendous benefit.

- 10 minutes: This length of meditation lightly grounds you. It's enough time for the body to begin to unclench and the mind to start shaping into focus. Even this short amount of time will have substantial effects on how you experience the day.

- 20 minutes: This is the most economical meditation length. This amount of time allows you to plant both feet on the ground and feel the ground touching you back. Your mind will reach a focused place and your body will expand. The increase in your awareness will be visibly obvious when you open your eyes.

- 30 minutes: Ah, now we're talking. This is how long I meditate each day. I find that it provides the same benefits as 20 minutes, but dials things in a bit deeper. To me, that bonus level of stillness is worth the extra 10 minutes.

Sure, setting a meditation timer can be useful for busy mornings. But I think there is a deeper answer to the question of duration. We can find that answer in the reason we choose to meditate at all.

We meditate to focus our minds, release negative emotions, relax our bodies, gain personal insights, and bring peace into our lives. The answer lies in the intention.

We should meditate until the peace comes. This sounds basic.

But as I mentioned, it's hard for people to resist overcomplicating simple answers.

Each day comes with a different amount of personal contraction. To stay open we need to meet the clenching head-on. Some days it's easier than others to reach a point where we feel focused, present, and expanded. On tough days we might need to meditate a little longer. The important thing is to get to where you need to be for today.

TIME IS NOT THE ESSENCE *of* MEDITATION. MEDITATION *is the* ESSENCE *of* TIME.

In meditation, we should sit and work with what we are holding in ourselves at that moment until our hands are free. This is how one lives lightly. Through honest and patient meditation, we can release what life gives us to carry each day. This freedom is what gives us the capacity to be filled by the present.

Thinking About Not Thinking

People have many misconceptions about meditation. One of the most common is that the goal of meditation is to have a mind without thoughts. This idea comes from a confusion of metaphors. When people who meditate talk about having a "clear mind," they don't mean that they have no thoughts. They mean they have more awareness of their thoughts. The "clarity" is an ability to view your thoughts with a touch of space so that you don't get wrapped up in them. A "clear mind" such as this allows you to be mindful of how you respond to your life.

It could be a little unsettling if you were to picture someone with no thoughts or an empty head. Sometimes, that idea is even enough to turn someone off meditation altogether. But what would a person without thoughts even look like? A sleepwalker? This is something we don't have to worry about because it doesn't exist. If you're conscious, you will have thoughts.

Before we get too carried away, let's take a quick look at what we know about thoughts. One of my favorite things to do on my podcast is ask a neuroscientist, "What is a thought?"

This question is usually followed by a small pause, a chuckle, and a judicious answer. The fact is that modern science doesn't completely understand what thoughts are. Science still has an incredible amount to uncover about how the brain works as a whole, much less where thoughts come from. We know that thoughts occur when neurons send each other electrical impulses. But why and how is still an answer to discover.

If we do not know what thoughts are, then how would we even go about cultivating a mind without them? It doesn't seem possible. Because it isn't. That's why meditating with the intention of emptying your mind of thoughts is so frustrating. Not only can it not be done, but it isn't even something you should be seeking to begin with.

You will probably feel like your mind is running wild with thoughts when you first try to meditate. You might even feel like you aren't able to meditate because there's so much going on in your head. Don't get discouraged. This is as normal as it gets, and actually, even more normal than you might realize. See, your mind is always that noisy with thoughts. Meditation has only allowed you to notice it.

When you first sit down to meditate, keep things simple and take it slow. Drop your expectations. Experience things for what they are. Sit with your eyes closed and breathe like you are sleeping. Focus on the feeling of your chest expanding and contracting. You'll notice all sorts of thoughts pop in and out of your head. Let them come. Then let them go.

IMAGINE THAT *the* **THOUGHTS** COMING INTO YOUR MIND *are* FLOWING LIKE *a* **RIVER.**

As your thoughts flow by, one will jump out and try to grab your attention. That's just your ego beeping, letting you know that you're still conscious. Take a quick look at the thought, acknowledge it, and release it back into the river.

What's interesting about mental chatter is that you don't actually have to do anything to get it to calm down. All you need is patience. As you continue to practice the basic exercises I describe, your mind will become less noisy on its own. Often, you'll find that your thoughts are more active for the first five to ten minutes of your meditation. That's your mind acting like a teapot, blowing off the pressurized steam of the day. Once the pent-up mental energy releases, your mind will calm down and your thoughts will become fluid.

There I Am, There I Am

Becoming more self-aware is an important step toward living a present-minded life.

There's always a lot going on in our minds and around our bodies. So much, in fact, that we can get swept up in the shuffle of it all. When this happens, we can become driven by compulsive stress and start making mindless decisions.

I'm going to share a few of my favorite awareness exercises with you. I hope these tools serve you as well as they serve me. They are a great way to wake up your senses, focus your attention, and feel more deeply rooted in your body.

You should do these exercises while sitting or lying in a comfortable position. Also, be sure you have no audio or visual distractions. In other words: Sit down, cut the music, and put your phone aside.

The first exercise is meant to get you in touch with the sensations in your mind and body. It is easy to ignore or grow numb to what we are feeling. This practice will gently wake up your senses.

There I Am

Take a few relaxing deep breaths as you settle into your resting position. Close your eyes.

As you continue to breathe slowly and calmly, direct your focus to the feelings on your skin.

Your skin is what separates you from and connects you to the universe. There is always something touching it.

Maybe you feel air moving across your skin or the warmth of sunlight. Relax and feel as much as you can on your skin until you start to feel that your skin is tingling.

Now, begin listening to every sound you can hear. Do you hear the wind blowing through the trees? Do you hear your own breathing? Perhaps you hear something faint off in the distance? Listen close and see how much detail you can pick up.

Next, begin breathing in and out of your nose. Feel the air tingling the edge of your nostrils as you breathe out and the inside of your nose as you breathe in. Focus on this sensation for a few moments and then try to pick up as many smells as you can. See if you can identify something new.

While sitting there, tuning into your senses, exhale a relaxing breath and begin feeling what it is like to be in your body. You are in your body and your body is right here.

With your muscles relaxing more with each exhale, try to let go of any clenching that remains inside of you.

IMAGINE THAT **YOU** ARE LIKE *a* TREE, PEACEFULLY BLOWING *in the* BREEZE.

Now, with your eyes closed, start tapping into the feeling that you are in your body. Feel your awareness pulsing in your head. When you identify it, quietly say under your breath:

"There I am, there I am, there I am, there I am. Here I am, here I am, here I am, here I am."

Repeat these phrases as long as you desire. Open your eyes. Feel that you are happening now.

The next exercise will help you connect with your surroundings. By doing so, you will feel more present in your body.

Settle into a comfortable position and let out a relaxing exhale. Close your eyes.

Imagine a video camera outside of your body. It is five feet in front of you and five feet above you. Imagine that you are looking at yourself through that camera.

Picture yourself watching what is happening in the room in real time. There you are. Sitting and breathing. Hold this image in your mind for several moments. Indulge in your imagination and enjoy watching yourself sit in peace.

Continue picturing what you look like through this imaginary video camera. Begin to notice the outline of your body. Then, start to notice all your surroundings. Let the outline of your body dissolve.

Imagine that you see your body merging with your surroundings. You are a part of what you are resting on. Your body is like a stalagmite growing up from a cave floor. It is an individual while still being part of the whole.

Sit with this image and relax into the idea of yourself as a connected expression of the world.

Open your eyes. Feel yourself in your body. Feel the way you're connected to where you sit.

Present. Here.

In the last exercise, we are going to strengthen our focus. Some parts of this practice might seem somewhat odd at first. But as you practice it, you'll notice that you have an easier time focusing on your daily life.

This exercise is like a gym for your mind. It builds the muscle of attention. The more you practice it, the stronger your focus will become.

As your attention gets stronger, it will be easier to observe and manage your thoughts. This skill is useful in stressful situations or when negative emotions are high.

Relax into your comfortable position while maintaining good posture. Take several deep and slow breaths.

Close your eyes.

Imagine a shape floating in your mind. Picture a sphere, rectangle, or triangle.

Give that shape a color. Now, make that shape get larger, then smaller. Next, make that shape change color. It can change color once, or several times. Then, change the current shape into another shape.

Sit with this exercise and slowly change the size, color, and shape of your object. Practice this until you feel that your focus has had a good workout.

Open your eyes.

Set a timer for ten minutes. Pick a single small object or spot that is eye level.

Stare at the object or spot, without losing eye contact, until the timer goes off. Feel free to blink, but do not take your eyes off the object.

After the timer goes off, relax your eyes and look around your room.

Does your mind feel more focused?

Can you concentrate on a single thought with more ease?

I suggest doing each of these exercises once a week. After only a few go-rounds you'll begin to notice a change in your awareness. Then, your mental presence will start surprising you in your daily life. In a moment when you might feel confused, you'll find that your mind feels sharp. While you're dealing with many things at once, you'll notice that it's much easier to keep it all straight in your mind.

At a certain point, you'll notice that these exercises have become easy for you. This means that you've developed these mental muscles. When you reach this point, you won't need to do these exercises every week. But, if you start feeling rusty, they will always be waiting for you when you need them.

Floating in Space

By the time our bodies finally land in bed at night, our mental switch is usually stuck in the ON position. The constant activity we're engaged in through the day builds up a momentum of doing. When we get in bed, our muscles are still tensed and our buzzing brains are on standby, waiting to jump at the next task.

The day is winding down and we need to wind down, too. Well, unwinding would be more like it. We can't get to sleep while holding the tension of the day. If we do, we won't sleep well. We'll toss, turn, and wake up throughout the night.

This relaxation practice is the one I noted earlier in the book. It's one of my favorite ways to unwind before falling asleep. It can be done anytime, but I especially like doing it after getting into bed and turning off the lights. You'll feel great when you're done.

Lie down in a comfortable and quiet place. Turn the lights off if you can. Make sure that you are lying on your back, with your arms and legs spread out to the sides. Keep your limbs loose and natural.

Close your eyes and begin taking deep breaths. Slowly fill yourself with an inhalation. When you reach the fullest breath you can take, let your chest fall. Don't try to exhale. Let go and allow the weight of your chest to press the air out.

Continue this style of breathing, and with each exhale, try to relax all the muscles in your body. Inhale again, and when you exhale, try to relax all your muscles even more.

Keep breathing this way, and with each exhale, try to relax your arms, legs, face, shoulders, back, and feet. Allow your body to soften.

This is a practice of letting go. Continue relaxing your body and releasing a little more each time you exhale. Do this for five to ten minutes and see how much you can let go.

Return to your natural breathing style.

Do you feel like you are floating in space?

This is a simple way to prepare yourself for sleep. You'll probably notice you feel better rested in the morning, too. We sleep better when we aren't tense. So, decompressing beforehand is quite helpful.

I can get the deepest into this practice if I'm laying down with the lights off and have nothing else to do. But, that doesn't mean you can't do it elsewhere. It comes in handy if you find yourself in a place where you can let go, like lying on your couch or sitting on a plane.

I like to make this practice into a game and see how much I can let go. I try to go deeper and feel like I am floating a little more each time. One day, I hope to startle myself by bumping my forehead on the ceiling.

The Mindfulness Gap

Mental chatter will start to fade after we get a little meditation practice under our belts. When the chatter quiets, we're left with much more mental space. Then, arising thoughts become streamlined and clear. They have room to breathe, which makes them easy to identify. This is one of the ways meditation makes us more aware of what we're thinking.

When you're aware of your thoughts, you are able to control which thoughts turn into actions. This allows you to break free from reactionary ingrained behavior. We often react to the world without considering the impact our actions can make. This leads to harmful words and choices that we wish we could take back. And a lot of times, we wonder why we did them at all.

Meditation creates a mental space that lets us respond to life instead of reacting to it. This is a truly invaluable skill to develop. When you're in a situation and feel frustrated, awkward, or scared, you can be aware of arising impulses. This awareness will allow you to let go of reactive negative behaviors before acting on them and reconnect with the present.

The following practice will show you the process of recognizing a negative thought and letting it go.

When you start to feel overwhelmed by negative emotions, let that feeling be an alarm. The alarm should act as a reminder to pause, take a step back, and assess the situation.

Take a few deep and slow breaths. Then, point your focus toward what you are feeling.

You will see that there is a space between what comes into your mind and what you decide to put into action. For example, you could feel an impulse to set this book down, but decide not to and keep reading. I call this space the Mindfulness Gap.

So, after you've recognized a negative thought and slowed things down a bit, take a look at the way you feel you should respond to the negative emotions. Will your response to your feelings create harm to yourself or others? If the answer is yes, do not put your response into action. Discard it into the Mindfulness Gap.

Think of this as a catch-and-release method for negative intentions. We can catch the negativity before it goes into the world and release it from our minds.

To sustain peace in our lives, we must maintain the peace around us. The only thing this costs us is selfishness. By being mindful of how we respond to our lives, we can reduce meaningless harm to others and ourselves.

Binaural Bliss

One of my favorite meditation tools is an audio technology called binaural beats. Essentially, it is audio tracks that contain long vibrating tones. The tones are often accompanied by simple sound textures to make them enjoyable to listen to. Usually sounds like rain or singing bowls. Binaural beats aren't songs per se, but more like extended audio environments. If I had to classify them in a genre, I'd call binaural beats functional ambient music.

Binaural beats are useful because they help get your brain into a meditative state. The tracks are also typically pretty long in duration—generally thirty minutes to an hour. This is great because you can listen to one without having to restart the track while meditating.

So, how do binaural beats actually help get you into a meditative state of mind? Well, let's take a quick look under the hood. When the neurons in our brains send signals to each other, they tend to pulse in rhythmic patterns. These repetitive signals are also known as brainwaves.

The speed of our brainwaves changes depending on the activity level of our mind. For example, when we're sleeping our brainwaves slow down. When we're in a full-on flow state our brainwaves speed up. The vibrating tones in binaural beats are set to a target brainwave speed. Then, as we listen, our brainwaves are entrained to the specified target state in the track.

Let me simplify what that means. Say you're feeling a little brain fog while you're trying to work. By listening to a binaural beat with gamma waves, you could help get your brain into a more focused state. Or, let's say you're trying to wind down at night. Listening to a binaural beat with delta waves would slow your brainwaves and help you calm your mind.

I've researched and created many binaural beats in my studio over the years. My favorite ones are a set that I made for meditation. They contain a special recipe of audio tones and sounds that have quite a magical effect on the way you feel. They help you settle into your meditation zone with a true ease. They're also good to use when you're feeling stressed and need to come back down to Earth.

I've made one available for readers of this book at www.cory-allen .com/nitwbeats. Give one a listen using headphones during your meditation sometime. I believe it will serve you well on your journey.

I'd like to note that the science on binaural beats is still young. There are a handful of good studies out there. Many of them report binaural beats effectively shift brainwaves in test subjects. Of course, I'm always interested in learning more. I want to understand exactly how binaural beats can make you feel the way they do. That's why I'm collaborating with a team that is testing my binaural beats in a neuroscience laboratory!

Polishing the Silver

Think of your mind as a piece of silver jewelry. When you go out each day, the silver gets exposed to the elements and tarnishes a little bit. It doesn't corrode enough for you to see with the naked eye, but layers are starting to build.

After a month, your piece of jewelry starts to lose its luster ever so softly. As more time passes and the silver continues to be exposed to the elements, it gets even more tarnished. Soon, the jewelry stops shining altogether. It becomes dull and listless. This is what happens to us if we don't take care of ourselves. We grind through life taking on a little more corrosion each day until one day we notice we've stopped shining. This happens to us all. The good news is that just like a real piece of silver, we can counteract our daily tarnish with a good polishing.

These exercises combine light visualization with basic breathing techniques. Don't worry if you have a hard time conjuring up the visualization aspect of these practices in your mind. Follow what comes to your imagination, no matter how large or small.

Let go of what you think a visualization should be and work with what is. There is no correct way. There is only your way and what works best for you. Alright, let's polish some silver.

Flushing Waste

Take a deep breath and visualize a bunch of black sludge inside of your body. This sludge represents all the emotional waste that has built up inside of you.

As you exhale, picture (and try to feel) the breath pushing the black sludge upward like a plunger.

See all the black sludge move upward and shoot out of a hole in the top of your head.

Take another deep breath and repeat this visualization. Do it as many times as you need to feel cleaned out.

It usually takes me about five to ten breaths to feel like I've gotten rid of all my sludge. In my visualization, I know I'm done flushing when the stream of black sludge leaving the top of my head turns into golden light.

Golden Shell

Take a breath in and relax the muscles in your body as you exhale.

Visualize radiant streams of golden light swirling outside of your body.

As you take a slow breath, imagine streams of golden light getting sucked into an opening in the base of your spine. Keep in mind that your inhale is creating the suction pulling light into the opening.

See and feel the golden light swirling around in your body. Take another breath in. As you exhale, picture the golden light forming along the walls of your insides.

It's like you are creating a golden candy shell on the inside of your body. This shell represents a restorative life force that is fortifying you from the inside out. Repeat the visualization with as many breaths as you need to feel restored.

Breathing Through the Heart

Take a good breath in and let a relaxing breath flow out. Begin to picture something in life you love. It could be a person, concept, animal, or specific memory. Anything that brings up the feeling of warmth and love into your body.

As you take slow and relaxing breaths, continue picturing what makes you feel loved. Gather the fresh loving feelings in your body and move them so they are concentrated over your heart.

171

Picture that you have an opening like a mouth on your heart. Breathe the gathered feeling of love into your heart. Try to feel, with each breath, that you are literally breathing into your heart instead of your head.

Sit with this practice, breathing into your heart, until you feel warm and radiant with love.

Breathe in Energy

Take a deep breath in. Visualize a fire growing around your heart. Let that fire represent the feeling of love that you have for the people in your life. Allow it to thrive as a blaze of compassion.

When you exhale, imagine the fire that surrounds your heart spreading from your chest. Then, visualize the warmth wrapping around your whole body like a blanket of love and peace.

Relax the muscles in your body with an exhale and use your next inhale to soak up the feeling that surrounds you.

Each of these exercises has a function that repeats in connection with your breath. It doesn't matter how many breaths it takes you to reach the intended state of feeling. Some days it takes a few more and some days it takes a few less. What matters is that you are sincere and get your mind where it needs to be. Like a dull piece of silver jewelry, it doesn't matter how many rubs of a cloth it takes to get it clean. What is important is that it shines.

SIMPLER *is*
ALMOST
ALWAYS
BETTER.

The methods and exercises I've shared are useful ways to work out your meditative muscle and explore different aspects of what meditation can be. Once you feel comfortable playing with them, I suggest working on what I share here as the meat of your practice.

My practice has become more and more simple over the years. I used to get obsessed with all the different ways I could twist and stretch my mind. It was fun experimenting and I learned a lot. Although, after a decade or so, it became less interesting. So I began removing the cleverness from my practice until there was hardly anything left. Underneath all the creative practices was a simple meditation that I call The Watcher.

This method is practiced by sitting and doing nothing. You sit on your cushion, close your eyes, breathe deep, and watch your mind. There is nothing more to it than that. Even the thought of following steps in a meditation exercise is doing too much. Your breath and calm, flowing awareness are all you need to sit with.

You are the watcher looking out upon the world. You watch the world look into you. There is no attempt to get involved with the transaction. Your attention grasps and refuses nothing. You are present and life is happening. There you both are.

You focus on breathing and watch your awareness flow like a river. This state of mind is the most beautiful and peaceful place. It is where the "I" becomes the all. It is the clear mind concept that you have been searching for.

After you get comfortable on the cushion, strip the bulk of your practice down until it is this simple. Sit. Breathe. Soften. Clarify. Feel your presence. Be.

Someone recently asked me how I would define a successful meditation practice. Of course, it's going to be different for everyone. It will even be different for the same person on a new day. But as I reflected on the question, I chose to answer it as completely as I could. So I thought: What does the fruit of meditation look like in daily life?

When you look from your eyes, while looking in at yourself, and witness the two touching, you are meditating.

STARTING YOUR JOURNEY TO NOW

You Will Find Your Way
There's a famous saying by Chinese philosopher and *Tao Te Ching* author Lao Tzu that states, "The journey of a thousand miles begins with a single step." Given that Lao Tzu said this about 2,500 years ago, it's safe to say that his saying has stood the test of time.

And with good reason. This quote is still repeated today because it teaches us something we need to be taught over and over again. Lao Tzu's saying nails a fundamental aspect of how to do something. Not just how to think about doing something, but to actually do it. He reminds us that no matter how big or small a task may be, we have to start all tasks the same way: with a single act of doing.

People are enthusiastic by nature. That's one of the things that makes us so effective. When our imagination floods with possibilities we get inspired and energized. Then, our whole purpose often becomes finding a way to bring our idea to life. But given that we have forty thousand thoughts a day, we tend to have a lot less to show for them than we could. That's because we get excited by the idea of change or innovation and want to see it appear before us immediately. When it doesn't, our enthusiasm starts to fade, and we move on to the next distraction. This leaves us stuck in a loop, feeling frustrated and confused about why our ideas aren't coming to life.

As Lao Tzu said, to get started with anything, you've got to take the first step. That's great advice that often leads to a new question altogether. Yes, to start, we have to take one step. But how do we keep going? Another single step. Then another. And another. I can't stress enough that to improve your life in any way, you have got to take small, consistent steps over time. A single act of doing. Every day. You aren't going to meditate once on Sunday night and wake up Monday morning a Zen master. It doesn't work that way and you shouldn't want it to.

The modern world has groomed us to expect instant gratification. That's fine here and there, but what we get fast leaves us just as quickly.

PATIENTLY
CRAFTING
SOMETHING
is the PATH *to*
TIMELESS
MASTERY.

And that's what you're doing when you work with what we've covered in this book. You are crafting yourself into the person you know you can be. A person who is present, connected, loving, and inspired. Full of wonder. Glowing. Alive.

So, you know you need to take small, consistent steps to create real, lasting change. But how do you know where to step next? This is where your imagination comes in handy. To know where to walk, you've got to be able to see where you're going. Think of your imagination as a flashlight that you can point at the dark road that lies ahead. Picture the change you'd like to see in yourself or in your life and then walk toward it.

Do you want to feel less anxious? Then imagine what you would look and feel like if you were more restful. See yourself there. I'll bet that coolheaded you eats healthfully, exercises, meditates often, and doesn't fill your head with static.

Do you want to feel more alive? Then picture yourself energized and bursting with wonder. See yourself there. You know that version of you travels to foreign countries, is open to new experiences, and isn't afraid to dive in and get their hands dirty.

Do you want to live in the present? Then visualize what your life would be like if you were awake and tuned in to the abundance of now. See yourself there. That you definitely embraces moments, soaks up the warmth of life, and quickly breaks free from distractions.

These are examples of how you can identify better ways of living. Imagining yourself as the person you want to be is like using your flashlight in the darkness. Your visualization shows where your journey can take you. The qualities you see in your imagined ideal self are the things you should work on first. They are your steps on the path to change.

Sure, the path is never without its bumps. You'll have to find your footing sometimes and figure out how to walk just right. Your shoes might get wet when you cross the river. This is good. It's the way it should be. You will learn most from the unexpected. It is all a part of the journey of self-growth. What's more important than anything is that you are taking steps. By taking responsibility for your life, you will find more than a path. You will find a direction. You will find your way.

Keep Yourself on Track

It's easy to get excited about something. It's just as easy to lose track of whatever that thing was. When that happens, we forget about what caught our attention and move on to what we click with next. We behave like this more than we tend to realize. One day we might get fired up about getting in better shape. The next day we wake up, eat a healthy breakfast, and buy classes at a gym. After a few days, we find ourselves tiring out and falling into our old habits again. Or maybe we decide we're going to play the guitar. We buy a nice one, too, because if we're going to do it, we might as well do it right. Then, after a few weeks of YouTube lessons, the guitar becomes the newest addition to our closet of forgotten things.

If this is you, don't feel bad. It's all of us. This behavior tracks back to the fact that our brains are always scanning in a search for new things. A lot of the time, we don't even lose focus because we aren't interested in our new pursuit. It's because we don't have reminders to bring our attention back to it.

How can you overcome this natural human behavior and make a real change that's important to you? By building reminders into your life. The most effective way I've found to do this is by sharing what you're focused on with the people around you. Take an idea from this book that tugged at your intuition. Make that idea your first single step. Think of how it resonates with where you're at in your journey right now and how you can apply it to your life. Then, apply it. Pay attention to the ways you begin to feel more present-minded. Catch yourself connecting with moments and really letting them soak in.

As you take the single step you've chosen, share your journey with your friends, family, and coworkers. Of course, I don't mean for you to overindulge and talk everyone's ears off. Casually share what you're thinking, the idea you're working on, and your results with the people around you. By doing this, you're planting reminders in the ecosystem of your life. It's like dosing your own water supply. When you share something new and interesting with people, they'll ask you about it again later. Because it's interesting!

Those curious check-ins from people serve a very useful function. They make you accountable to them and yourself. And there's no better way to stay focused than to be accountable to the people close to you. Our natural instinct to perform and be there for our tribe is powerful. It wakes us up, gets us energized, and inspires us to keep going.

WHEN YOU BETTER YOURSELF, YOU BETTER *the* PEOPLE AROUND YOU.

A present, clear, open, and compassionate you will be of great service to everyone you know. What better inspiration could you ask for?

Open Up the Moment

We often develop our presence by practicing mindfulness at home in simple ways. Doing this is a useful step. Our lives will be richer if we start each day by engaging with our morning coffee. A mindful ritual like this feels private, special, safe, and just for us. While this is a great way to get started, we don't want to restrict our mindfulness practice to our home. It's important to remember that you can open up and migrate those personal mindful moments. You can make that feeling wide and spacious until it spreads across all of your experiences.

There's nothing wrong with taking small steps toward mindful living in a private way. That's how I did it at first. But please don't stop there. I don't want you to miss out on the full transformative power that present living has to offer. After you've become comfortable being present at home, try being more present at work. When you're effortlessly mindful around your friends, try being present with your family. If you take calming breaths while standing in line, then try feeling the warm water roll across your hands as you wash your dishes. There are endless opportunities for you to experience more presence in your life. All you have to do is keep looking for them.

You Live Well When You Love Well

I had the pleasure of speaking with Frank Ostaseski a while back. Frank's a remarkable person. He is a pioneer in end-of-life care,

Buddhist teacher, and founder of the Zen Hospice Project. He has dedicated most of his life to helping others in the final moments of theirs. While speaking with Frank, I felt something coming through him that I hadn't felt before. Picture when your heartstrings get pulled so tight that you're at a loss for words. Then, imagine sitting in that intense feeling. That's what it was like to speak with Frank. I actually started crying out of nowhere while we were talking. His resting affirmation of life was so moving that it simply flooded my emotions.

While we were talking, a fascinating and important question came to my mind. So, I asked, "What matters most to people in the final moments of their lives?" It felt right to ask Frank this because he is uniquely qualified to answer. He has sat with thousands of people while they were dying. He listens to them, gives them love, lends them his physical strength, and helps them let go of fear. After I asked, it didn't take him long to answer. He replied, "Did I love well?"

We tell ourselves that we aren't going to take life for granted. You and I both want to live life to the fullest and not let time pass us by. That's a great thing to aim for. And I hope all of us do. But sometimes, we can lose sight of what that idea realistically means.

Adventurous vacations and memorable nights out are certainly full experiences. So are big professional wins and sensational meals. But these kind of things are temporary and rare. That's what makes them special. Perhaps there's a broader way to think about living life to the fullest. One that doesn't miss the rest of the mountain by only looking at the peaks. What if we spent less time fantasizing about what is rare and more time feeling what is here? A vacation lasts a week.

THIS
MOMENT *is*
FOREVER.

By taking to heart what I've shared in this book, you can get in touch with what surrounds you in each moment of your life. You can also get in touch with the you that is experiencing it all. By being present you can feel each breath, release your fear, and let a smile wear you. It only takes a single step each day for you to get closer to now. It is all here. It is waiting for you to wake up to it. I know you can do it, too. You are doing it right now.

So take your first single step, my friend. Begin your journey of a thousand miles. Along the way, never forget that it's all going to be OK. Trust your compass. Be yourself. Love well.

ACKNOWLEDGMENTS

Thank you for reading this book. I hope it treated you well and linked some of your beautiful experiences.

Endless gratitude to Anna Geller, Meredith Maples, and Kevin Kaiser. This book would simply not be what it is without your invaluable feedback. By talking deeply and honestly with me about the writing process, you helped me understand how to unite the "I's" inside of me so that I could write authentically, with my heart, mind, and intention in balance. My humblest of thanks also goes to Marian Lizzi at Penguin Random House for believing in this book and offering her wisdom along the way.

I continue to be humbled by the unwavering belief and support from Christopher Schenk, Mike Vernusky, Adam Corrigan, and John F. Simon Jr. You have believed in me so deeply from the start, encouraged me, and worked so hard to help manifest my passions into reality. I'll always be grateful and hope this book delivers what you saw in me.

My gratitude to my podcast listeners is beyond words. But I will say this: Hello, my dear Astralites! It's an honor to spend each week with you, stretching our brains and opening our hearts. Truly, without your support, this book would not have been possible. You amazing, deep, and loving souls have contributed more to my life than you'll ever know.

I look forward to growing together for years to come.

Thank you to my friends and fellow podcast hosts for keeping it real, making me laugh, and being a bottomless source of fresh thoughts to chew on. In a world that is seemingly designed to dull your senses, you keep me sharp, bright, and waiting for the next punch line.

Meredith. You find all of the answers I cannot. You see the puzzle pieces I don't even realize I should be looking for and hand them to me without hesitation. Your authenticity, love, intellect, and patience continue to inspire me to be better than I was yesterday. Thank you for being you—a force of nature—which is responsible for the glow in my eyes.

ABOUT THE AUTHOR

Cory Allen is an author, podcast host, meditation teacher, composer, and audio engineer from Austin. On his podcast *The Astral Hustle*, he finds ways for us to live with more wonder and less suffering by speaking with leading experts in mindfulness, neuroscience, and philosophy. *The Astral Hustle* has been downloaded millions of times and was featured in *The New York*

Credit: Courtesy of the author

Times. Cory has taught thousands of people how to meditate with clear and concise methods in his online meditation course *Release into Now.* He is also a distinguished music producer who has released more than a dozen albums and engineered hundreds of records for other artists.